D0821434

REPRINTS OF ECONOMIC CLASSICS

SOCIAL REFORM & THE CHURCH

Also published in

REPRINTS OF ECONOMIC CLASSICS

by JOHN R. COMMONS

THE DISTRIBUTION OF WEALTH [1893]
LABOR AND ADMINISTRATION [1913]
PROPORTIONAL REPRESENTATION [1907]
RACES AND IMMIGRANTS IN AMERICA [1924]
A SOCIOLOGICAL VIEW OF SOVEREIGNTY [1899-1900]
TRADE UNIONISM & LABOR PROBLEMS *First Series* [1905]
TRADE UNIONISM & LABOR PROBLEMS *Second Series* [1921]

JOHN R. COMMONS & JOHN B. ANDREWS

PRINCIPLES OF LABOR LEGISLATION 4TH EDITION [1936]

JOHN R. COMMONS *Et Al*

HISTORY OF LABOR IN THE UNITED STATES,
4 VOLS. 1918, 1935

SOCIAL REFORM

&

THE CHURCH

BY

JOHN R. COMMONS

[1894]

Reprints of Economic Classics
AUGUSTUS M. KELLEY PUBLISHERS
New York 1967

First Edition 1894

(New York: Thomas Y. Crowell & Co., 1894)

Reprinted 1967 by
AUGUSTUS M. KELLEY · PUBLISHERS

Library of Congress Catalogue Card Number

66 - 21663

PRINTED IN THE UNITED STATES OF AMERICA
by SENTRY PRESS, NEW YORK, N. Y. 10019

SOCIAL REFORM

AND

THE CHURCH

BY

JOHN R. COMMONS

PROFESSOR OF ECONOMICS AND SOCIAL SCIENCE, INDIANA UNIVERSITY
SECRETARY OF THE AMERICAN INSTITUTE OF
CHRISTIAN SOCIOLOGY

WITH

AN INTRODUCTION

BY

PROF. RICHARD T. ELY

NEW YORK: 46 EAST 14TH STREET
THOMAS Y. CROWELL & COMPANY
BOSTON: 100 PURCHASE STREET

CONCORDIA UNIVERSITY LIBRARY
PORTLAND, OR 97211

COPYRIGHT, 1894,
BY
THOMAS Y. CROWELL & COMPANY.

CONTENTS.

INTRODUCTION.

I⊤ is but a few months since PROFESSOR COMMONS gave us an important contribution to economic theory in his " Distribution of Wealth," a work which, in my opinion, is destined to exercise a decided influence upon the development of economic thought. The present work fitly supplements the earlier volume in several directions. It is more popular in character, and is calculated to exercise a more immediate influence upon practical affairs.

The character of the topics discussed in this volume is significant, because political reforms, as well as social reforms, are urged from an economic standpoint. ADAM SMITH said long ago, if a rod is bent too much in one direction, to make it straight we must

bend it as much in the other; and this saying illustrates the attitude of social reformers
towards politics. Earlier in the century there
was a tendency to give undue importance to
mere political reforms. The Chartists in England directed their attention to political reforms, and many of them seemed to think
that these alone would improve the condition of the masses. The Christian Socialism
of Maurice, Kingsley, and others in the middle
of the century was, to some extent at least,
a protest against the exaggeration of political
measures.

Since that day, the interest in politics on
the part of the advocates of economic reforms
has greatly diminished, because it has been
perceived that politics is concerned with the
outward form and not directly with the substance of things. The interesting questions
of the day, so far as they have taken hold of
the masses of mankind, have been socio-eco-
nomic questions, not political questions. The
rod has been bent too much, perhaps, in the
other direction; and now we may hope that

it is becoming straight, since a comprehensive treatment of the social problems of the day shows that we require improvement in political conditions, in order to supply us with a better political machinery for carrying out various purposes with respect to the amelioration of social conditions.

Civil service reform is an administrative measure which has popular economic bearings not sufficiently considered heretofore, because the larger aspects of civil service reform have been neglected by those who have been most prominent as its advocates. But we begin to hear much of direct legislation by the people as seen in the use of two Swiss institutions, the Initiative and the Referendum. Still another political measure with important economic bearings is proportional representation, which is so excellently treated by Professor Commons.

Next in importance to the direct instruction and information conveyed by these essays, is the significance which they have on account of the fact, already mentioned, that they unite political and economic reforms, looking at the former from the standpoint of the latter.

It gives me much pleasure to welcome this work and to commend it. Opinions may differ in regard to the views presented in this work, as well as in Professor Commons's "Distribution of Wealth;" but there can be no doubt that they both afford an excellent stimulus to popular thought, and that they are calculated to awaken men to the true importance of popular questions of the day, and to help get us out of the ruts into which we are so likely to fall. It is a time when we need vigorous thinking, clear thinking, and a right spirit ; and all these are found in the works of Professor Commons.

RICHARD T. ELY.

PREFACE.

THE following essays, except the last one, were read originally before audiences distinctively Christian. Some of them appeared subsequently in print. "The Christian Minister and Sociology" was published as a leaflet by the Christian Social Union in the United States. "The Church and the Problem of Poverty" appeared in the *Charities Review* of June, 1893. "The Educated Man in Politics" was published by the *Indiana Student*, a monthly periodical conducted by the students of Indiana University. The essays on "The Church and Political Reforms," and "Temperance Reform," were read before a sectional conference of the Evangelical Alliance at Chicago, and will probably appear in the published proceedings of that meeting. The paper on "Municipal Monopolies" is printed here for the first time. "Proportional Representation" was read at the World's Congress on Suffrage, and is here presented as supplementary to the essay on "The Church and Political Reforms."

JOHN R. COMMONS.

INDIANA UNIVERSITY, BLOOMINGTON, IND.

November, 1893.

THE CHRISTIAN MINISTER
AND SOCIOLOGY.

SOCIAL REFORM AND THE CHURCH.

THE CHRISTIAN MINISTER AND SOCIOLOGY.

Sociology is properly the science which deals with society as a whole. It co-ordinates all the special social sciences, such as ethics, politics, and religion. It studies society as an organism, and shows how other social sciences investigate simply different phases of that organism. The sociologist studies the individual man, not as a separate particle, but as an organ intimately bound up in the social organism. It is this organic nature of society which alone furnishes the reason for a science which can be called sociology. The fact that I am dependent for the clothes I wear, not on the individual of whom I bought them, but on millions of individuals working together throughout our whole nation, with more or less harmony, teaches me that it is this organism, society, which determines my weal or woe. If I can devote myself to literature and science, if I can worship God in the midst of beautiful and inspiring surroundings, it is because society cares for my bodily wants and leaves my mind free for nobler things. Society gives me my opportunities; I myself am responsible only for the use I make of them. This brings us to the special significance which sociology has for the Christian minister and the Christian believer. Although sociology deals with all phases of society, yet there are practical problems to-day which give it a special application. Society gives us opportunities; yet there are great classes of society, including millions of individuals, from whom society withdraws everything that we deem worthy of even the name of opportunity. This is the problem of sociology with which the Christian has most to do : What are the relations of society as a whole to the unprivileged classes? What is there in the social organism that produces these classes? Can anything be done to give them opportunities for a higher life? Can they be educated to make good use of improved opportunities? Whose duty is it to give them these opportunities and to teach them how to use them?

In order to put this matter clearly I will present four propositions which lead logically up to the special purpose of this paper.

FIRST — *There is a social problem. In the last analysis it is none other than the distribution of wealth.*

This is the social side of all our social problems. Our social classes are based on private property and education. But property holds the key. The educated classes themselves are dependent for their livelihood upon those who control the property. As for the classes who depend wholly on their daily wages, access to land and capital is their only means of life. They must find an employer. The man with-

out an employer is a vagabond and an outlaw.
What are the results of this condition? On
the one hand is great wealth, bringing great
luxury and extravagance, great haughtiness and
little thought for the trials and privations of
the unpropertied. On the other is insecurity
of employment and a servile dependence enforced by the whip of hunger, more inexorable than all tyrants. The moral effects of this
condition are just what we should expect. Pauperism has become a subject worthy of scientific study. Crime has increased. Intemperance has become frightful, because life is a
dreary burden of work, with no future of relief,
and food is poor in quantity and quality. The
home is being disrupted, because the working
people are crowded into open tenements and
the family cannot meet its daily wants without
the help of wife and children. And these evils
do not tend to right themselves. We cannot
placidly rely on any abstraction of natural
selection to wipe out crime and intemperance
and to preserve the family. Rather do these
evils multiply. Evolution is not always devel-

opment upwards. A new race of men is being created with inherited traits of physical and moral degeneracy, suited to the new environment of the tenement house, the saloon, and the jail. I know there are well-to-do persons who decry such statements as these, who prefer to write and read books on the progress of the working classes, who say that the world is growing better. It is true that a part of the world is growing better, that many workingmen are in better circumstances than were their fathers; but these are the skilled and well-organized workingmen. The great mass of workmen, when we consider all their circumstances, are no better off than they were thirty years ago, and many are worse off. But, after all, men do not compare themselves with their ancestors, but with their contemporaries. You cannot appease a restless workman by telling him how much better off he is than was his simian progenitor. What he feels is his dependence on his fellow-man, who is growing richer every day upon the fruits of his own poorly-paid toil. This, then, is the first revelation of

sociology — that there is a social problem growing out of the distribution of wealth ; that
through the organic nature of society this
problem ramifies in all directions, and appears
in the tenement house, the saloon, the jail, the
poorhouse, and that under the operation of
existing forces this problem is daily becoming
more intense.

SECOND — *Christianity is the cause of our
social problems.*

The spirit of Christ, working in an evil world,
has, indeed, brought not peace, but a sword.
Thus it has always been and always will be.
Why should we look upon the conditions I have
described as in any way objectionable ?   Why
not simply say, " There are profound laws of
nature which cannot be changed, which cause
these differences.   Let us eat, drink, and be
merry, because it is none of our business"?   No,
we look upon such conditions as a serious problem.   But there would be no problem at all,
were it not for our ethical and Christian ideals,
which abhor injustice and inequality.   Before

the Christian religion had spread through the world, slavery was considered as the natural lot of four-fifths of mankind. This is the reason why slavery was no social problem. Slaves themselves accepted their conditions as wholly fitting. But Christ, without attacking directly the institution of slavery, undermined its foundations when he taught the brotherhood of man and the moral dignity of every soul before its Heavenly Father. Slavery could not long exist in a world where the religion of Jesus told every man that he was his brother's keeper. When religious equality became accepted as the faith of mankind, there could be no peace until our laws, our constitutions, and our courts recognized political equality. To-day the problem is the same. The man who has a birthright in heaven equal to that of any other man must not remain on earth the dependant of his brother. The sword of Jesus will not be sheathed until every man has an even chance here below. Economic equality may never be obtained, and, indeed, it would be undesirable, because the needs of all are not alike. Our needs depend upon our education, our culture, our ability to make a good use of worldly goods. But equality of opportunity, free scope for development of such gifts as we have, are the logical conclusions of Christianity. To be tied to the earth by the daily necessities of life when others, with no greater needs, are wasting the fruits of our toil, is the essence of inequality and injustice. Workingmen themselves have eagerly accepted this ideal. But right here they bring a serious charge against the Church of Christ. They say the Church begs them to be quiet under their wrongs in this life, with the hope that they will have their reward in the hereafter. No charge is urged more bitterly than this. If it be true, the Church has utterly perverted the teachings of Jesus, and we have the striking anomaly, a source of constant discord, that while Christianity has awakened higher ideals of life among the masses and made them restless, the Church has opposed the realization of those ideals in the life where they most are needed.

THIRD — *It is the failures of Christians that perpetuate and intensify social problems.*

I believe that there is but one solution for social problems. It is the bringing of the two extremes of society together, the wiping out of mutual misunderstandings, and the promotion of mutual acquaintance of each other's feelings, wants, and hopes. In other words, it is the introduction of love into social relations. The present division of classes results in exclusiveness, ignorance of social conditions, and consequent hate. Both sides need to know by personal contact the conditions of the other. Both sides are to blame. Wage-workers misunderstand the rich and hate them. The well-to-do misunderstand the workmen and fail to give them sympathy. The fault of this evil condition is in the Christian Church. Christians possess the wealth and intelligence of the country. It is their duty to make the first advances. They are in the world to obey the command of Jesus, "Thou shalt love thy neighbor as thyself." This does not mean to make all the money you can by close bargains with your unequals and by cutting down employees' wages, and then to use your money to build a college, or subscribe to some philanthropic society which doles out alms to your neighboring paupers. It means to go yourself, to get acquainted with your neighbors, to pick out some hard-worked mechanic, some shiftless pauper, some slave of drink, and love him. Christians have not loved their neighbors. They have hired somebody else to love them. They have left it to the women. Thus they have intensified social antagonisms. They have made it impossible to understand the grievances and the wants of workingmen. They do not study these grievances and these wants, because they do not love the unprivileged and neglected classes.

FOURTH — *The failures of Christians are due to the failures of Christian preachers.*

The Christian ministers are the leaders of Christian activities as well as Christian thought. They give direction to these activ-

ities. The success of foreign missions is due
to the frequent exhortations of Christian ministers. Monthly prayer meetings, with reports
from the foreign field, and the general stimulus
to this line of work, are due to the activity of
the Christian pastor. The minister should do
the same for social missions. If he should
take a hearty interest in social questions, if he
should hear the bitter cry of the home heathen,
if he should take it upon himself to present
their cause, soon the Church would follow in
his steps, and no longer could the blame for
social ills be laid at the doors of Christians.
Christianity is the only solution for social
problems, and society is waiting for the Christian minister to lead the way.

There are two things which the minister
must do at present. The first is to show the
facts. This is the urgent need of the hour.
His congregation must learn that there are
ominous social wrongs to be righted. The
preacher should be a student of social science.
He should study books. A small library, wisely
selected for him by some sociologist, and

costing from thirty to fifty dollars, would be found amply sufficient for beginning his work. But equally as well should he study persons and families. He should find the facts by personal contact. Then he should present facts prayerfully. Let him avoid sensationalism as he would sin. He will succeed in this if his purpose be truly to benefit those whose cause he presents.

The second thing for the preacher to do is to show the responsibility of Christians for these conditions. We have got beyond that age of materialism which ascribes social conditions to workings of so-called natural laws which man cannot modify. Social conditions are the result of the human will. This human will finds expression in two ways — in the every-day activities of individuals and in legislation. These two facts are the causes of social conditions, and they are simply the manifestations of the human will acting individually or collectively. In our country this means the Christian human will; for it is the Christians whose wealth and intelligence control legislation, and whose wealth and intelligence in private affairs outweigh all other private influences. You may say that there are also natural conditions which are the causes of social conditions, such as the fact that a man must work for a living, or that great law, which is the corner stone of political economy, the law of diminishing returns. True, there are natural conditions, but natural conditions have become of inferior significance. A century ago, or among uncivilized tribes, they were all-important. But the machinery and inventions, the aids to production, all that go to make up the wealth of our country, are so abounding that if the American people seriously wished it, there would not be an able-bodied pauper or a tramp among us. If we wished it, there would be no involuntary idleness, which is the prolific parent of voluntary idleness.

Now, I believe it is the duty of Christian ministers to convict sinners of their sins. They must first convict them before conversion is possible. Here is the great sin of

Christians — we do not acknowledge that we are our brothers' keepers ; we do not love our neighbors. We pass by on the other side. We are " exclusive." Here, then, is the crucial duty to the minister, a hard task, indeed, but one that Jesus met ; and he has shown us how to meet it. Christians must learn that they, and they alone, are responsible if the ills of society are allowed to continue. And the preacher is the man to tell them so.

With the conviction of sins comes the cry, " What must I do to be saved ? " Here the preacher must be the guide. He must show men how to love their neighbors. With this practical application of Christianity is involved the answer to the question, " How much should the work of the preacher be modified in the direction of sociology ? " He cannot go too far in showing facts or responsibilities. But he can go too far in practical work. These social problems will soon become political problems. The preacher ought not to become a politician. He should do as Jesus did ; work on the hearts of men, give them right purposes, show them

the evils to be overcome and the end to be
reached, and leave to them the ways and means
for bringing about the needed legislation. But
outside of politics there are many practical
activities which the preacher should lead, and
thereby show his congregation how to be saved.

First—and most important of all—he should
lead his people in becoming friends to the
neglected classes. He should himself become
acquainted with two or three such families.
He should be acquainted with the police court,
the jail, the workhouse, and the almshouse.
He should induce every member of his church
to take one family or one individual, and to
love that family or individual. They should
not limit their work to the poor, the criminal,
and the idle alone, but to all who are out of the
Church, and whose necessities compel them to
live a modest life. Where the poor are concerned, let the preacher resolutely stand against
giving them alms. The neglected classes want
not alms, but friends ; and what a vantage
ground the friend has over the almsgiver !
He only can get at the hearts of people whose

lives have been spent in trying to deceive philanthropists. As a friend he should not limit himself to the single work of converting to Christianity. He should learn from social science that the body must be saved before the soul. He should give help in every way that is needed — help to get employment, help to economize earnings. He should show them how to buy their clothes and food, how to cook, how to read books, how to enjoy themselves, in fine, how to live. If he love them, he will see where is their greatest need.

The preacher should see to it that every church member becomes a social missionary. It is usually taken for granted when a proposition like the foregoing is made that the men are to furnish the money and the women to do the work. A heresy more pernicious has never rent the Church. What these people need is often simply business qualities, the ability to save money and to apply their labor more effectually and systematically. Where the husband is most to blame for the poor condition of his family, no woman visitor can have any influence. It needs an energetic, prosperous business man with a heart of love to put a backbone into a man and help him along the lines of his own success. Moreover, the rich man needs this personal contact as much as the poor. He can never have proper ideas of philanthropy, can never learn to love his brother until he knows him. And the main object of the mediating power of Christianity will not be attained if the well-to-do members of the churches are not brought into contact with the opposite extreme of society. Here, then, is a perennial subject for the preacher to bring before his congregation : their responsibility for the neglected classes, and methods of meeting that responsibility.

Second — I do not think it too much for the minister to devote one-half of his pulpit work to sociology. By this I mean not merely the line of exhortation and practical methods just indicated, but also sociology in its broadest sense, as a science, showing the fundamental relations and principles of society. Sociology has rightly been said to be one half of religion ;

theology is the other half. Each deals primarily with the individual man, but with the individual in certain relations. Theology considers
man in his relations to God ; sociology in his
relations to his fellow-men. If, then, ministers
instruct their hearers about the nature of God,
should they not instruct them equally about the
nature of society ? If their exhortations be
directed towards love for God, should not equal
attention be given to love to man ? If they
show them how to love God, should they not
show them how to love man ? The Bible gives
abundant precedents for this kind of preaching.
What a wealth of social philosophy you can get
from that book ! What a never-failing source
of inspiring sermons can be found in Christ's
social and economic teachings !

It is true that ministers do devote a very
great part of their work to enforcing the duty
of love towards our fellow-men. But this is
not enough. There is a good love and a bad
love. The greater part of the history of Church
charities is simply a history of pauperization.
People need not only the heart of love, but also

the knowledge wisely to guide their love.   This
can be derived only from the science of sociology.   The effects of social activities are far-
reaching and occult.   No off-hand philanthropy
can excuse itself with the plea that the heart is
right, therefore God will care for the results.
Such a philosophy makes simply fanatics.   Here
social science can come to our aid.   The great
object of sociology is to teach us how to love
our neighbors.   As a science, it is already developed so far that its precepts may be taken
as a safe guide.   The preacher who has at hand
the investigations of its leaders would find that
one-half his time is not enough to reveal the
wealth of sound practical love to man which they
contain.   I have sometimes thought that no
better use could be made of the Sunday evening
service than to devote it to a course of sermons
on sociology.   Let the minister clothe in Christian eloquence the results of science.   He
should begin with the organic nature of society,
showing that it is based properly on Christian
ethics ; then the nature and functions of the
State as a mighty force in furthering God's

kingdom and establishing righteous relations among men ; then the family and the home as the centre from which radiate all the good and all the evil of our society, where the heritage of love or of hate is handed down to future generations along with life itself. From the State and the family, as the two fundamental institutions of society, we advance to the social problems of the day. To all of these Christian ethics should be applied. Marriage and divorce, intemperance, crime, pauperism and poverty, wealth and luxury, are all special phases of the social organism and have their roots deep in the substance of society itself. These can be presented by the minister in a form at once popular and scientific. Throughout all these discourses he should keep in view the main object of Christianity, to bring the extremes of society together in brotherly love. The ablest discussions of sociology will be mere word-making, if they do not tend to this result. But I believe that a community which should have in its midst weekly ministrations of this sort for a year or more, would be stirred to its foundations and moved as never before by the love of humanity.

I long to see the day when the leadership in the social movements of our time will be taken from the lawyer and the newspaper and given to the Christian minister. We cannot expect to have a society based on righteousness so long as our social philosophy is given to us by editors and lawyers. They are put forward to favor special interests. But where is the advocate of the masses, of the great brotherhood of man? Where is the truly judicial mind, whose purpose it is to bring to pass the kingdom of God on earth? The Christian preachers have failed to see their vantage ground, or, seeing it, have failed to take it. They have confined their thoughts to individual righteousness, and have failed to take in the broad field of social righteousness. The people are eager for knowledge on social questions. They need to know what righteousness is, not merely for the individual, but for society. So long has dust been thrown into their eyes by passionate partisans, that we may now see them turning in disgust and scepticism to their own turbulent impulses. I do not believe the masses of the people are wholly wrong at heart. They have simply lost faith in their would-be leaders and know not where to turn. Here is the opportunity for the preacher of social righteousness —not the man who makes special pleas, but the man who understands the nature of society and believes in God. In the pulpit is where he belongs; and once a week, more powerfully than editor or lawyer, he can build up about him a community where every man will love and help his neighbor, where happiness will be diffused, and righteousness be easier than sin.

Third — It is impossible to separate the strictly pulpit work of the minister from his general religious and social work. The pulpit is simply the place for the public expression of his every-day work. The topics which he discusses there grow out of the needs of his congregation and community, as he finds them day by day. The character of his pulpit work depends upon the character of his Church work.

Consequently, it would seem that the Church ought to be organized on such a plan as to give the minister opportunity for social study and social work. By this I mean that the Church ought to take on a popular, week-day character. It should be a centre for amusements, athletics, debating clubs, and reading circles. It should be a people's church in the fullest sense. This idea is becoming a familiar one. In order to carry out successfully a course of sermons on sociology, the preacher needs to stimulate the reading and conversation and co-operation of his parishioners. He needs to bring in outside elements, workingmen and others, for mutual conference. He needs to make his church a recognized centre for social and helpful activities. There should be a church library on social and economic subjects. Prayer meetings should be places for reports from church members as to what they have done for families or individuals whom they are loving. Many other features of Church work will readily be suggested to the preacher who attempts to introduce thoughtful sermons on sociology and to inspire his people with the social missionary spirit.

To sum up this matter of the character of the Church and its life as well as that of the preacher's social and pulpit work — they should all be determined by the great feature of Christianity which I have already emphasized, its mediating power in drawing social classes together. Here is where Christianity strikes at the root of social ills, and there is no other power in the community that can so strike. We must all come around to the simple gospel of Christ, and we must apply this gospel in its right proportions, realizing that religion is love to God, and sociology love to man, and on these two hang all the law and all preaching.

THE CHURCH
AND THE PROBLEM OF POVERTY.

THE CHURCH AND THE PROBLEM
OF POVERTY.

THE problem of poverty is not an isolated problem. It is a part of all the social questions of to-day — of the questions of labor, of crime, of intemperance. On account of the organic nature of society these problems are laced and interlaced — they act and react on one another. The causes and remedies of poverty can be comprehended only through an understanding of its relations to the whole social organism; and this involves a thorough acquaintance with human nature, with the laws of psychology and biology.

It is in this broad aspect that I believe it most profitable to consider this question. And it will be found that the solution of the question of poverty — if there be a solution — will be also the solution of the questions of labor, the family, city government, crime, intemperance.

Furthermore, the problem of poverty — or any other social problem — to my mind has no significance except as it is a religious problem. Man is made in the image of God. His possibilities are divine ; and it is an appalling sight to see the godlike crushed out of such a being by poverty, by crime, by intemperance, by his social and industrial surroundings. When the Christian Church awakes to the daily life in the dark places about her, and understands the essential religious nature of the problems of labor, poverty, monopoly, then may these problems be put in the true way of solution.

Modern science teaches the unity of human nature. Psychology, physiology, sociology, all the sciences which treat of man, declare that the two elements of which he is composed — body and soul — are not antagonistic but interdependent. Yet to-day many of us are holding to that mediæval doctrine of the eternal opposition between body and soul. It was a doctrine which in its day of ascendency sequestered good men as ascetics and hermits, and left bad men in unhampered control of practical affairs.

To-day this doctrine leads the Christian Church to preach salvation only for a future life — salvation for the soul apart from the body. Oppressive and unjust conditions in this life are looked upon as ordained means of grace to discipline the soul and turn its longings towards the hereafter.

As a result of this doctrine, the Church shrinks from contact with practical life, and has looked complacently on while poverty has increased, crime has leaped forward, intemperance has become a giant. I do not say that this is the attitude of the whole Church to-day. But the Church's ignorance of modern science, and her bias toward the old dogma, still appear in the way in which she attacks only the symptoms and results of social disease, and not the causes. The intemperance question is to be solved simply by abolishing the saloon — regardless of the fact that intemperance itself is the result of profound social conditions. Sunday labor is the only labor problem attacked — and that only in its spectacular and relatively harmless occasions — and the irresistible economic necessities of modern civilization which compel Sunday labor are overlooked. Corrupt city government is ascribed, not to its real causes, but to the sinfulness of politicians — whereas the fact is that in city politics all our political and social machinery is so arranged that the best men are, as a rule, barred from success.

The sciences of man to-day teach us the mutual harmony and affinity of body and soul. They show how these shape and re-shape each the other. There is no alienation, there is no antagonism between them. The soul is simply the expression and flower of the body. It is that in the body which experiences all the thoughts and emotions, the ideals and aspirations. These may be good or bad. They may be emotions and ideals of love or hate, of faith or infidelity, of hope or despair. But, whatever they are, they depend upon the body. Bodily wants are the primal and indispensable wants. With the infant and the child they are the only wants. And how eagerly loving parents attend to the physical wants of the little one, rejoicing as their reward in the slowly budding signs of affection and aspiration — the beautiful tokens of the unfolding spirit.

But how shall this soul unfold and develop? Sociology, based as it is upon the sciences of biology, tells us it is through that universal law of life — adaptation to environment. Adaptation is direct and indirect; the first is effected through use and disuse of faculties ; the second through heredity. Thus the individual, both in his body and his soul, in the process of generations becomes fitted to his environment.

Now, it is society that furnishes the environment of the individual. Society determines the conditions under which his physical and spiritual powers shall be permitted to develop. Society creates great social classes, and assigns the individual, even before his birth, and on through infancy, youth, and manhood, to one of these classes. For generations before his birth, and again through the plastic years of childhood, his particular social class is shaping and conditioning his physical and mental powers, his appetites, emotions, and ideals. In our day these social classes are based to a large extent on property. It has been possible, heretofore, for individuals to pass from one social class to another ; but these class lines have become more rigid, and the individual, if his lot be in the unpropertied class, is destined, as a rule, to remain there. His economic resources determine, by a resistless pressure, what shall be his social environment. I will indicate briefly some of the main characteristics of this social environment as it has developed in our day, and show its influence upon the individual.

The first is that condition of the working classes which can be characterized as none other than wage-slavery. By wage-slavery I mean the dependence of one man upon the arbitrary will of another for the opportunity to earn a living. This is the essential evil in the wide extremes of wealth of to-day. It is the ownership of all the opportunities of labor — the factories, the railways — by single corporations, or corporations acting as one, and their power to discharge workingmen for any reasons they think fit. This is an imperial power, and may become a tyranny. It can be remedied only by recognizing in man as one of his inalienable rights, along with life and liberty, the right to employment. We are apt to think that the rights to life and liberty are aboriginal and natural, and we marvel at those who talk of new rights as innovators and disturbers; yet there was a time when our ancestors recognized neither the right to life nor to liberty. Among primitive peoples enemies were slaughtered as a matter of course, like wild animals. Old and decrepit people, the sick and feeble, the defective infants, were exposed and sacrificed simply because they were a burden. It was only through centuries of moral development that the right to life became a sacred right.

And so with the right to freedom. When slavery was substituted for slaughter it marked an ethical advance, for it helped men to realize the right to life. Slavery taught habits of industry and made possible the growth of civilization; but in time, when Christianity taught

ideas of man's equality and the sacredness of
the human soul, slavery could no longer exist.
Man's moral ideas had advanced too far. Freedom has now taken its place. But the Christian who believes in the fatherhood of God and
the brotherhood of man, and who studies the
working classes at first hand, can see that
there is still lacking a true and manly freedom.
Robert Burns understood the secret when he
wrote : —

> "See yonder poor, o'erlabored wight,
>   So abject, mean and vile,
> Who begs a brother of the earth
>   To give him leave to toil."

And a friend of mine, an educated man, who
has given years of time and strength in the
cause of the laborers, has told me that now he
understands the problem that Moses faced for
a lifetime when he tried to lead a nation of
slaves forth to freedom. The workingman of
to-day, unless protected by his powerful labor
union, is slavish in his instincts. I speak of
laborers as a class, for there are noble exceptions. He is distrustful, jealous, incapable of

co-operation, treacherous to benefactors and fellow-laborers, and an eye-servant. These pitiful qualities of his soul are but the natural fruit of his unstable, dependent conditions of livelihood. How is Christianity to reach such a man with its noble qualities of truth, love, honor, fidelity, manliness, until it has first created for him those physical conditions of life and true independence out of which such qualities can spring?

Again, what can we expect to be the soul-life of the millions in our country who cannot find regular honest work to do? The seriousness of the problem of poverty to-day is not that there are greater numbers of poor, relative to the total population, than ever before, but that greater numbers are constantly on the verge of poverty. The fluctuations of modern industries, the panics and crises and industrial depressions throughout the world, are constantly shoving armies of men over the poverty line. And even in our best of times there are more men to work than places to work. The problem of the unemployed is a problem

of Christianity. Involuntary idleness and irreg-
ular employment are the antichrist of to-day
that drives men and women into crime, intemperance, and shame.

You may say that the problem of the unemployed is the problem of the inefficient. Not
wholly true, for there have always been the
inefficient; but lack of employment in our
country dates from the close of the civil war
and the panic of 1873. Yet suppose your
contention be true — does it not prove that
the Church has not taken hold of religion in
earnest until she has studied the causes and
remedies of inefficiency?

What, next, can the Church expect the spiritual possibilities to be of men who are doomed
to long and exhausting hours of labor; who
work seven days in the week, and have no
holidays or vacations except those granted by
pitiful accidents and sickness? It is not only
absurd, it is cruel, to expect such men to become Christians. Yet do we hear the Church
or the ministers crying out against this worse
than chattel slavery? I should have thought

we should have heard the whole Christian Church in America rise in one indignant protest when the fact was brought out, in the strike of Buffalo switchmen, that men had been compelled to work in the Buffalo yards for thirty-six consecutive hours. Yet the Church and the ministry as a whole looked on in indifference, or else rebuked the men for anarchy and for stopping the wheels of commerce. Had the Church done its duty beforehand, and made any effort to know the life of workingmen, as Jesus did, there never would have been occasion for a strike, because hours of labor would have been limited to a point consistent with Christian manhood.

Again, there can be no hope for God's kingdom on earth except through the stability and purity of the home. This is the one social institution for which Jesus Christ gave us definite regulations. Yet, to-day, among the poorest classes, home is a travesty. The mother must work to compensate the father's enforced idleness and low pay, and her children come into the world with feeble bodies, broken

nerves, and moral impotence.   It has been said
that to educate a child you must begin with
his great-grandfather.   More to the point is
it that if you would have a people intelligent,
moral, and Christian, you must relieve their
mothers and grandmothers from poverty and
excessive toil.   The home is the place where,
most of all, environment tells.   Overwork for
women and children is the physical basis for
crime, intemperance, and vice.   The youth, the
man, or the woman who has grown up in a
home — or the mockery of a home — such as
this, can never escape from the prison of his
own faltering body.   His soul, as long as its
physical house endures, is incapable of stead-
fast, noble impulses.   The appeals of Christianity are incomprehensible to him.   And yet
who has heard that the Church, in its assemblies, its pulpit, its press, or its hundreds of
committees or sub-organizations, has taken up
systematically the cause of the women and the
children workers ?   No, her voice has not been
heard for reforms that threaten profits.   Her
appeal has been for men to share their profits

with her — to build her magnificent temples and swell her missionary accounts.

Other features of the modern environment of the working classes might be mentioned. While there are many hopeful features, the majority are depressing. I turn now to one or two specific reforms, which the science of sociology has indicated, and note the reception the church has accorded them. Crime has increased in forty years five times as fast as population. Yet ministers of the gospel know little of that divine science, penology. Our city workhouses to-day contain prisoners who have been committed from fifty to a hundred and fifty times, and very little thoughtful Christian effort is made toward their regeneration. And all this occurs in the same city and within sound of the minister's voice. Yet the ministers go their way, week after week, in ignorance of these sin-sick souls — in prison, and they visited them not. Now, scientific penology has already pointed out the way firmly, yet gently, to cure them ; yet how few are the ministers who know anything about prison reform.

The case is similar with intemperance. It is treated solely as a sin, to be exorcised by repentance and punishment ; but science is showing that it is also a disease, largely the result of industrial conditions — a disease to be treated like insanity. And ministers exclaim against such conclusions, as tending to weaken the springs of duty, and to free men from responsibility ; therefore they strike only at the symptoms of the disease, the saloon, — a crude kind of social therapeutics. Christians, along with others, have made wonderful progress in utilizing the results of physical science, steam, and electricity, but they know little of the results of social science.

I have insisted, as a lesson of science, on the unity of human nature, and the priority of man's physical organism in all the walks of life ; yet I do not rule out the eternal verities of religion as they are emphasized to-day, — the sinfulness of man, his need of conversion, the transforming power of faith in Christ and immortality. Indeed, I believe that true science shows these to be essential to social regeneration. Man, after all, is not an animal : he is a being of aspiration ; he rises by his efforts toward the ideal ; he is not to be lifted up from beneath and carried into the realms of manhood and righteousness, but he is to be lured and won and inspired by longings for faith, hope, love ; yet he is at the same time the creature of his environment. The inexorable earthly wants for food, clothing, shelter, press daily upon him. If he be confident that these will be regularly supplied in a self-reliant way, and if in supplying them his bodily and spiritual powers be not basely exhausted, then he may rise above the animal and reach out for the noble joys of the soul; then, and then only, can religion touch him.

This is the fundamental error of the Church. She has made her spiritual appeal to men who could not possibly do more than supply their earthly wants, and has made no effort to help them where most they needed help. Is it any wonder that they revile her ? The Church has left the radical religious question, the betterment of social conditions, to atheists and

agnostics. Is it any wonder that efforts at social reform hitherto have risen no higher than
materialism and mammonism ? The Church is
to blame that she has withdrawn from the field
where God and duty and the example of her
Saviour called her to lead, and left it to those
who sought only the loaves and the fishes. In
the noble science of sociology, peculiarly her
own, she is not the pioneer, but the camp-
follower.

I have pointed out some of the principal
evils in the industrial environment of the working classes, and have shown the duty of the
Church to consider and remedy them, and the
failure of the Church to do so. It will be said
that I overlook what the Church is already
doing; no, I recognize gladly the efforts of
Christians in many places, especially in many
of those overworked and under-appreciated
down-town churches, but I affirm that my
strictures are true for nine out of every ten
churches and ministers in our land.

Now, I should prove a fruitless and carping
Jeremiah if, in addition to what I have already

said, I were unable to point out how the Church is to meet these problems, and to show that it is possible for her to meet them. From what I have said, it follows that the first thing to do is for ministers and church workers to get information, and to learn general principles. Let them study the science of sociology in all its branches, as they have studied the science of theology. Magnificent work has been done in this science, and its best general and special treatises are safe guides to the student. The causes of phenomena in sociology, as in every other science, lie beneath the surface, and cannot be discovered by the beginning student from his own original observations. He needs the guidance of trained observers and philosophical thinkers. With this in view church libraries on sociology should be carefully selected, and the books circulated among the congregation. The minister should be a guide to the reading and study of his parishioners. Frequent addresses could also be secured from specialists in charities, penology, the family, labor, monopolies.

But books and lectures can do little more than stimulate and guide. The essential method is to come into actual contact with social conditions. For this purpose there is no better way than to adopt the methods and join in the work of the modern scientific charity. A charity organization society means far more than its name indicates. It is not a society for dispensing alms, but a society for investigation and friendship. It is organized Christian love, reaching to the very root of all social questions. A charity organization society touches every social problem — the problem of labor, of the unemployed, of long hours, of women and children workers, of city government; it offers the only true way of getting at the facts which I have dwelt upon. The man who has assisted in this work for even a short time can speak with assurance. He knows the actual conditions whereof he speaks. I should not feel so strongly nor know so surely the terrible power of capital over labor, through the denial of the right to employment, had not work in a charity organization society brought me into contact with individual cases.

There is no position so good as that of
friendly visitor in a charity organization society for getting beneath our industrial system,
and understanding its true significance for the
hearts and souls of men. Such a position furnishes the best possible opportunity for labora-
tory work in the science of sociology; it
is the doorway to a real knowledge of social
problems.

If I could prescribe a course of study for
every minister and church member, I should
say, enroll as friendly visitor in your local charity organization society. Have one or more
families assigned to you, get acquainted with
them, become their friends, help them in every
practical Christian way except giving alms.
Then, in your weekly meetings with other
friendly visitors and the society's trained sec-
retaries and agents, compare notes and cases,
and discuss plans for reforming individual cases
that are practical under existing circumstances.
Thus you learn conditions and evils and their
causes; you learn what society is doing to meet
the evils ; you get an idea of what ought to be

done, and you see how urgent and tremendous is the problem.

Does it seem a hopeless matter to enlist the churches in this kind of work? In German cities every citizen is liable to be drafted by the municipal authorities to serve as a friendly visitor, with severe penalties if he refuses. Cannot our Christian church members, filled with the life and example of Christ, gladly do for his little ones these services of scientific love? There is to-day in every American city a pressing need for such workers. And I see no other way for the Church truly to awake to her duty and her opportunity, and to learn what to do and how to do it.

THE EDUCATED MAN
IN POLITICS.

THE EDUCATED MAN IN POLITICS.

THE current recommendations for the educated man to participate in politics are vague. The preacher, the editor, the reformer, urge him to go to the caucus and see that good men are nominated. Again they tell him to be the independent voter and the scratcher, — the man who is always looking out for something to oppose, — until he is driven to believe that his only part in politics is that of a self-righteous and negative scold.

But there is something better for the scholar in politics. Not that he should fail to be independent. This follows necessarily, if we assume that he does his own thinking. But there is a difference between independence and stubbornness. Independence is positive and progressive. Stubbornness is negative and stationary. Independence recognizes that political parties are large, cumbersome, unwieldy machines. They accomplish nothing perfectly. Their one inseparable feature is compromise. The independent man should recognize himself as a very small part of an immense enginery. He should try to make his influence positive for good, but he should remember that good in politics is accomplished only by moving massive bodies.

But what is politics? And what is there in politics that should call for the thought and action of the educated man? Is politics a struggle between office-seekers, or between classes, or sections? Practically it is all of these. But to the educated man it is something far deeper. It is assumed that the educated man is the Christian man. It may not be that he is a signer to any formal creed, but if he has rightly grasped the fruits of the highest education he must accept the ethical teachings of Christianity. The Christian is here to benefit his fellows in every possible way, — physically, mentally, spiritually. Two ways for doing this are open to him. First, in his private life he can be attentive to the highest interests of those about him, and by joining with others can form private associations for the benefit of those who are in ignorance, weakness, and oppression. Thus arise our great charities and benevolences, the home and foreign missionary societies, the temperance unions, the churches and Sunday-schools, the associated charities and prison-reform associations. All these are the efforts of individuals.

Now, a very little work of this kind soon teaches that there are powerful underlying evil forces, which individual effort cannot reach and overcome. Evil forces and men are everywhere, and have the same opportunities and liberties as the good. Individuals and associations cannot cope with them. They are increasing in power and terror every day. Consequently, the educated Christian soon finds that he must look elsewhere for some *supreme force* that can wipe out these evil forces. This is politics. Politics is the co-operation of citizens for employing the sovereign power of government to crush the evil and promote the good forces of society. Government rests ultimately upon force. It speaks not with tongues, but with the mighty arm of the law. It is the greatest power for good that exists among men. Where individual and voluntary effort fails because it cannot say "Thou shalt," and "Thou shalt not," individuals can co-operate in politics and summon to their aid the irresistible power of the State, whose commands must be obeyed.

Thus the two ways in which the educated man can use his powers to benefit his fellows are the individual, or voluntary, and the political, or compulsory. The two are complementary. The voluntary method is first. It can accomplish much. But in most important points it fails. Here the compulsory method must enter, and fill out the measure of good which the voluntary cannot complete.

What, next, should be the standpoint of the educated man when he enters practical politics ? We have our answer already. He should take the standpoint of the working classes, that is, of the class whose only means of livelihood is the daily labor of their hands.

There are several reasons for this position. The wealthy and educated classes do not need his help. Our governments, local, State, and national, have hitherto been controlled in the interests of the capitalist and land-owning classes. Laws on our statute-books are framed in their interests. Also, the educated classes have been simply the hangers-on of the wealthy. Where do we find the fifty-thousand-dollar lawyer except defending the interests of monopolies and trusts? Does the powerful lobby — so powerful that it is called the third house — does the lobby that attends our councils, legislatures, and Congress, labor in behalf of the hand-working masses?

But while these upper classes do not need their help, the wage-working classes do need intelligent and friendly counsel. They need powerful influences to be brought to bear for their benefit upon legislatures, courts, and executives. They cannot employ a lobby, they cannot adequately influence lawyers, and they themselves must attend plod-dingly to their hours of toil. Where can they look for help but to the educated man, be he lawyer, teacher, minister, or merchant? And where can the educated man put in heavier blows for his fellows?

Besides, the prosperity of the employing classes depends upon that of the wage-earning classes. The latter make up four-fifths of our population. They furnish four-fifths of the markets for what the manufacturer, the mer-chant, the farmer, has to sell. A merchant prefers a prosperous customer to a poverty-stricken one. The former buys more goods, of better quality, pays higher prices, and doesn't have to be dunned every week in the year. So with all the business, employing, and capitalist classes. Their highest pleasure should be to see the bulk of their purchasers, the wage-earning class, get constant work, high wages, and intelligent, moral habits of expenditure.

Lastly, the burden of unjust laws and cor-rupt politics falls more heavily on the wage-earning classes than on any other class. It is this class which is nearest the margin of poverty. If the pressure of bad laws settle down a little more heavily, it crowds great numbers of them just over that terrible dead-line. Pauperism, crime, intemperance, are the result. If other classes lose in one field, they gain in another. A rich man has wide interests and wide opportunities for investment. If one fail, he can withdraw from it and develop the others. An educated man can turn his hand and head to many different things, and he is in demand from all sides. But a workingman has but one skill. Daily wages in a single narrow field of industry is his only reliance. The great majority of our population is destined to be always wage-workers. The large prizes and high places are for the few. A railway can have but one president and one general manager; but it must have ten thousand manual wage-earners. Only one out of ten thousand can possibly rise to the highest place; the others depend upon their wages; and if wages fail, their whole life is shattered.   Moreover, the wealthy man can lose a thousand dollars and it means no more than the cutting off a luxury or two; but with a poor man, it means the loss of his home and the breaking up of his family.   Defective laws, corrupt administration, dilatory courts, often prove of advantage to the well-to-do.   But they crush the poor beyond hope.

Taking all these facts into account, the educated man in politics should place himself at the standpoint of the laborer.   Laws should be framed and administered, and courts should be guided, with his interests first in view.   The educated man is the one to see that this is done.

Having determined his standpoint, how shall the educated man begin the practical work of politics?

The first thing is to get acquainted with the working classes.   Visit them in their homes and workshops.   See how they live.   Find out what they need to make their homes happier.   Are the wife and children compelled to work in order to eke out the family income?

Are the hours of work long and the factory surroundings unwholesome ? All social reforms must centre in the home as the pivotal point, if improvement is to be deep and lasting. Let the educated man become an active worker in some charity organization society. The object of such a society is not alms, but friendship. It aims to detect the idle and fraudulent, and to help the honest and unfortunate. Its visitors go regularly to the homes of all who need help, they find out what are the defects of such homes and the circumstances of the inmates.

But how will this assist the educated man to take part in politics ? A few examples will show. A friend of mine has been visiting a colored family. The head of the family is a hard-working, sober man. Several years ago he managed to purchase a little home on long payments. After it was all paid for he suddenly discovered that he had not a good title, and now his home has been taken from him and his hard-earned savings have been lost. My friend immediately began to inquire whether it will not be possible to devise a plan for making real estate titles as safe and simple as the title to a suit of clothes. He soon discovered that there is just such a plan in force in Australia and in certain provinces of British America, and that it is being investigated in some parts of our own country. He is now working with others to bring this plan before the legislature of his State. If it can be adopted, many a wage-worker will be encouraged in habits of thrift and love of home, besides the stimulus it would give to business in general.

Again, the associated charities of a certain village have been looking up some wayward boys and sending them to the reform school of their State. The association sends its agent to the school annually to look after the boys. The agent discovered that a Democratic appointee had greatly improved the reformatory, and was teaching the boys useful trades far better than had ever been done before. The agent made his report ; and when a Republican governor came into office, a petition was circulated and signed by the best Republicans of the village, requesting the Republican governor to retain the Democratic superintendent in office. Thus have friendly visiting and charity organization reached out for civil service reform in politics.

Innumerable like cases could be cited. I myself first awoke to the selfish, irresponsible, and fearful power of great corporations when through charity organization work I came across a man who had the following experience. He had been vainly hunting for work for several months. At last he was promised work by the foreman in the stables of a street-car company, and told to come around the next morning at three o'clock. So anxious were he and his family for the work that his wife sat up all night to be sure to waken him in time. He reached the stables and went hard to work. At about ten o'clock in the forenoon the foreman told him his work was unsatisfactory and that he might leave. He protested and asked the reasons, but could get no answer. In a dazed condition he walked out. Later he asked one of the other men if he could tell him why he was so suddenly discharged. The answer came that he had neglected to do as all the others had done — pay the foreman ten dollars for the job, and promise, besides, to pay him a dollar a week out of his wages.

Now, corporations are creatures of government. They could not exist a day if the sovereign power of the State were not back of them, giving them the rights to buy and sell and hold property, and to act as a single aggregation of capital, with all the enormous power which this implies.

If the State creates corporations, it can determine the conditions of their existence. It can provide that no corporation can do business which works its employees more than eight hours a day, or which does not guarantee to them the right of employment without fines and perquisites so long as they honestly do their work. Stockholders in corporations at present can easily evade their responsibilities to the working people who make their money for them. They can leave such matters to subordinate superintendents and foremen, and

they themselves need never interfere in the
management so long as dividends are fat.
Here is a subject for far-reaching political
action. In the very nature of the case nothing but the coercive power of government can
avail. And here is a noble opportunity for the
educated Christian to become a practical politician for the good of his brothers.

Other means may be mentioned, besides
friendly visiting, for becoming acquainted with
the working classes. A good way is to join a
labor organization, especially the Knights of
Labor, wherever there happens to be a district
or local assembly. Most educated men would
be admitted, for the only classes excluded are
lawyers and saloon-keepers. In all cases the
educated man should get acquainted with those
who are near the poverty line or just over that
line. This includes the great mass of un-
skilled, unorganized day laborers. It is here
where defective and unjust laws accumulate.
This marginal zone of poverty includes nearly
all women wage-earners; and here is the field
of the educated woman in politics, — to join

working-women's unions, or help organize such, and then to work for laws to protect women and children workers.

Now, in joining such unions or in going among such people, let the educated man put away all thought that he is going as an instructor or guide. He is first of all a learner, and only a beginner at that. He is perhaps full of book knowledge, which he has acquired in college. There he has learned from the illustrious standard political economists that the working-men are all wrong in their demands ; that they are going contrary to nature, and, since God made nature, they are even atheistic.

But instead of finding that they are all wrong, he will find that they are more nearly all right. Though they know little of abstruse books, they are in daily contact with things, and soon feel where the shoe pinches. There is some deep reason in the boycott, in the refusal to work with non-union men, in the complaints against women and child labor, against the introduction of machinery, and against contract and prison labor. What these reasons

are the books have not taught; and the educated man does not know. If he studies them
at first hand, he may not be convinced by the
workingman's arguments, but he will begin to
comprehend that these are real evils which
they seek to avoid. He may conclude that
the evils can be remedied only by reaching
causes deeper and more remote than even
the men themselves are able to see; but he
will see that the fundamental social wrongs
of which they complain can be remedied only
through politics.

He will see, perhaps best of all, that it is
not through the great national and spectacular
questions which divide parties that the welfare
of the workers is to come. Protection and free
trade, silver and foreign affairs, are of little con-
sequence. But the vital political questions are
to be settled in his own village or city, and in
his own State. Here is where corporations are
created and their rights and duties defined;
here is where prison and contract labor, women
and child labor, and hours of labor, are to be
determined. Here is where popular education,

temperance, economy, and virtue are to be promoted, so far as this can be done through politics.

In concluding, we may restate some of the points just made in order to show how the educated man may be, not a negative and stubborn element in politics, but a positive element for good.   First, by enlisting with the working masses, he is on the side of the voters.   And if he steadily refuse to become a candidate for a salaried office, he gains their confidence and avoids the name of demagogue.   Second, he discovers that evils which are complained of to-day do not have their source in a single cause, but rather are a network of causes and effects.   Long hours and low pay are causes of intemperance and poverty, and intemperance and poverty are causes of long hours and low pay.   Consequently the educated man should not become enamoured of any single reform.   If the working people and political parties are not ready to move against his pet evil, let him take up that reform which seems at the time most likely of success, and to his surprise he will find that he has helped to remove one of the causes for the very evil which he himself has seen most clearly. Then is he in a position, through the confidence he has won and the common-sense he has shown, to point the way to what he himself considers important.

And, lastly, let the educated man have a due sense of his own insignificance and ignorance, realizing that he is an atom in a huge machine, and that other atoms know as much, perhaps, as he does.

THE CHURCH
AND POLITICAL REFORMS.

THE CHURCH AND POLITICAL
REFORMS.

I AM to speak upon the relation of the Church to political reforms. I shall consider, first, What part has politics in the salvation of the world? Second, Why does politics fail in its mission? Third, How can politics be made an instrument of social reform? Fourth, What should be the attitude of the Church toward politics?

There is a new idea abroad regarding the relation of the Church to society. The Church should not content herself with saving individuals out of the world, but should save the world. *Society* is the subject of redemption. And this not for the sake of any abstraction called society, but for the sake of the individuals who compose society. It is being recognized that the way to save individuals is not merely to pick out a few through the agencies of temporary excitement, and thus to obtain a confession of sin and a profession of faith, but it is to gradually develop all that is highest in every son of man, whether he be a believer or not. This is the meaning of Christ's profound saying, that God "maketh his sun to rise on the evil and on the good, and sendeth rain on the just and on the unjust ;" that is, on those who profess him and those who reject him. The Church must do the same. But the Church has worked on the principle that it can do nothing for the unjust, that is, non-church-members. It can build up Christian character only in those who have already come into the fold.

A deeper knowledge of humanity shows this to be fallacious. Man is a social animal. He is a part of a living, growing organism. He receives life handed down by generations of ancestry. He grows up amidst an all-pervasive pressure of beliefs, opinions, sentiments, habits, and industrial conditions. He is, therefore, the creature of his social class. If the members of this class be weak in body, mind, nerve force, and will power, and, therefore, the slaves of their surroundings, he will be also. Hence the reformation of society is a problem of *ages*, not merely a question of picking out individuals after they are born, but of saving them generations and centuries before they are born.

There is no remedy known which will cure society in a day or a generation, or even a century — it is the physiological problem of breeding. And the longer the life of the individual the longer the problem of experiment. Heredity is potent in any lasting social reform. But heredity can be modified by modifying environment. Almost nothing can be hoped from an adult generation whose parents have lived in surroundings of poverty, crime, and laziness, and whose childhood has been similarly nurtured. Little can be expected even from children now living in such surroundings. The Anglo-Saxon displaced the Indian from the land of his fathers, and so in society a large part of the question of reform is not how to reform, but how to *displace*, the baser elements.

At the same time the environment has a most powerful influence on individuals. Given a man with good ancestry, and place him from childhood in such degraded home and neighborhood surroundings as exist in every city, town, and rural district of our land, and he will retrograde. His children will come into the world still lower in the scale, and the evil environment will cumulate its results from generation to generation. It is from the world about us that we get all our soul experiences and our character building. But it is not the physical world that teaches us. It is our social world. Life is interpreted to us by those with whom we live. If their lives are narrow, over-worked, ignorant, aimless, how can ours be better? And what will be the gain to take a few individuals — even a few children — out of such surroundings, when the surroundings themselves remain? Hundreds of children are thrust in for every one that we can get out. The only remedy is to reform the surroundings, — and this means to reform society from top to bottom. The exclusiveness, luxury, ostentation, of the upper four hundred are but the glossy side of the shield to the herding, deprivation, and ignominy of the four hundred thousand who support them, or feed upon them.

In a matter like this small measures effect no results — they even make matters worse. By large measures I mean not revolutionary, but *scientific* and fundamental measures. Science means knowledge, profound knowledge, of forces and tendencies. Without the science of sociology there can be no reform of society. Christianity means a purpose, an enthusiasm, a devotion, a faith, a love for humanity. Love and knowledge, Christianity and science, theology and sociology, must unite to save the world.

Now, the first thing needed is a careful study of social conditions, and the formation of measures for reform. Human nature must be studied. Social classes must be understood. The characteristics of the defective, dependent, and delinquent classes should be the familiar knowledge of every Christian. Information about labor, monopolies, taxation, money, ought not to be accepted on tradition, but by study at first hand. Evils must be comprehended before reforms can be suggested. Then reform experiments everywhere ought to be examined and compared. Reforms cannot be entered upon without a basis of experience. And in nearly every field this experience is now at hand. Take the matter of profit-sharing. This is a far-reaching, Christian reform. And it is no longer a matter of dreams and theories. Careful students have collected the methods and results of several hundred experiments. Successes and failures have been noted, and their causes analyzed. He who adopts this policy now is like the machinist who builds after an approved pattern, rather than like the inventor who risks all to gain all. So with other reforms. So far advanced is the science of sociology, based upon comparisons of practical experiments everywhere, that almost the only thing needed now is the diffusion of this science among the people at large.

But there is a radical defect of machinery that stands in the way. As soon as a policy of reform is set upon in whatever field, it is found that in order to be fundamental and adequate, the laws of the land must be modified, or new ones introduced. Government is the only supreme authority among men. It is the only institution which can make its plans comprehensive. It is the only means whereby refractory, obstructive, and selfishly interested elements of society may be brought into line with social progress. Run over in your mind all the reforms agitated in these days, and see that nearly every one requires legislation. Child-saving, prisons, charities, taxation, monopolies, money, co-operation, every effective measure for the advancement of society, turns upon the formation and administration of laws. Laws must be framed and executed all the way from those which are merely permissive up to those wherein the government absorbs and monopolizes the affair in hand.

" This work of Christianizing our governments," says Dr. Gladden, " seems indeed a herculean labor; but it is one of the most immediate and most urgent of all our Christian duties." Yet the reasons which Dr. Gladden gives for Christianizing politics are among the minor and incidental reasons. There are indeed very few Christians who comprehend the strategic position held by government as the key to all social reforms and the Christianization of society. Take, for example, that large class of reforms connected with child-saving. This work is mostly voluntary on the part of private societies. But private societies can do nothing without the co-operation of the legislative and the administrative authorities. The rights of children must be defined and enforced as against the rights of parents. The laws of adoption and wardship must be modified in harmony with these newly recognized rights. The legislature is the only authority which can create new rights and provide for their enforcement. Then, reformatory institutions must be provided and maintained by the State according to wise principles. It is from the lack of proper legislation that the children of the poor are to-day being overwhelmed by crime and vice, and a race of vagabonds is being brought up in our midst.

So it is with temperance reform. There is no Christian work which needs more thoughtful and scientific treatment. But nothing can be done without proper legislation. Almost every reform you can name is to-day blocked at the doors of municipal, State, and Federal legislatures.

What kind of men do we send to our law-making bodies to attend to this most fundamental part of Christianizing society? I need not describe them. The people and the newspapers are fully informed regarding them. The serious fact is that they are mostly new men. One-half to two-thirds of the members of our legislative assemblies are serving their first term as law-makers. Our laws everywhere are being made by a majority who never before tried their hands at law-making. Many of them, too, are incapable. They have been elected because they were amiable nobodies, and perhaps had declared for a reduction of taxes. They of course know little about the progressive interests of the State. They are not alert to reforms that are needed. They give little evidence of scientific knowledge of sociology, of economics, of penology, of public finance. They know not what other States and countries are doing. They even have no conception of a Christianized society. They ridicule such things — unless a powerful political interest happens to be concerned. They are concerned with rivalries and spoils.

In modern society we do most of our work by proxy. We carry division of labor to the extremest limit. We cannot attend to all matters ourselves in so complex a civilization. But for that work which we delegate we try to select men appropriately equipped. When you employ a physician you seek out a man of sobriety, intelligence, and scientific knowledge of medicine. When you go for a tailor or a shoemaker, you enquire for a man who has learned his trade, and who knows how to measure and fit. Your minister of the gospel must be adapted by character and training to his work. But when you choose the men who do the most far-reaching and fundamental of your delegated duties — those services which are the prerequsite of all social activities, and without which efforts to save society are but salve for dyspepsia — strangely enough, you select from the ignorance, the vice, and the incapacity of your community.

With such a body of men elected to legislatures and councils, it is not to be expected that the real law-makers will be found among them. The true legislators of America are unknown to the constitution and the law of the land. They are self-appointed, private organizations which have grown up with gigantic strength in the past thirty years. The veritable law-givers, who stand behind the scenes and pull the strings which control the tools on the floor of the legislature, are the managers of the political party machines and the lobby. These are the organizations which have grown up under the forms of our free and representative institutions, and have engrossed the substance of power. To the people remain the husks and the bonfires. The lobby is the

creature of the great corporations and the organized financial and saloon interests.   It includes the brightest and most capable men in
the State.   The party machine is the organized
clique of spoilsmen who feed upon the public
storehouse.   And naturally enough the machine and the lobby are one.   They include the
same individuals.   They sap the corporations
and the moneyed interests on the one hand,
and they dictate to the law-makers and distrib-
ute the spoils on the other.

I do not say that there are no exceptions to
my description of legislative assemblies.   In
every legislature and municipal council are to
be found able, clean, and honest men, sincerely
striving to do their duty.   But can any one
show such a man who will consent to remain
in a State legislature or a city council for more
than one or two terms?   If he is not ousted by
machine methods he will soon voluntarily aban-
don his venture.   He is made to feel that he
is out of his place.   He can have no influence
over his fellow legislators.   He therefore de-
clines re-election ; and if his constituency is an

exceptionally good one, another man like him will be elected, only, however, soon to follow his predecessor.

In the main, it is as I have described it. The lobby and the machine are the rulers to-day of the American people. If we are so foolish as to entertain dreams of what we fondly call the Christianizing of society, at the very threshold of our hopes we are scoffed at by these usurpers of the citadel. Here is where the first movement upon the forces of social wrong must be made. The key to social reform is political reform, and the key to political reform is the legislative department of government.

It is the custom nowadays for newspapers and those who are alarmed at our political prospects to berate the intelligent and Christian classes of the community for keeping out of politics. These classes are in a majority. It is assumed if they would only attend the primaries and go to the polls, they could easily control the elections. But in this complaint, two important facts are overlooked. Politics is a business. The successful politician must give his whole time to the profession. The primaries and the polls are the least part of his work. There must be professional politicians who act as leaders for political interests, just as there are professional doctors, lawyers, teachers. The true problem is not how to do away with professional politicians, but how to get better professionals. The second fact overlooked is that our system of elections is so contrived that reform politicians cannot get elected. We elect a single candidate by a majority or a plurality vote. This narrows the choice down to the two candidates representing the two great political parties — that is to say, representing the two machine organizations, and the professional politicians of those parties. A candidate free from the rule of the machine cannot be elected unless he can get a majority or plurality of the votes. But, as everyone knows, reform movements must grow gradually from little beginnings, and therefore a vote for a third candidate is a vote thrown away, or rather, a vote for the machine of the opposite party. Now, the reform elements of the country are not always united. " There are several ways of moving," says Sir John Lubbock, in this connection, " but only one way of standing still." Consequently our system prevents reform elements from having almost any political influence whatever. What is needed in order to reform our politics, and give a fair field to all classes of social reforms, is a system whereby these reform elements can elect representatives and aldermen *by less than a majority or a plurality vote.* That is, they should elect representatives in proportion to their numbers, and not be compelled to wait for representation until they can secure a majority of the voters in one or more districts. That is to say, the key to social reform is some effective kind of minority or proportional representation.

This is a political reform which has already been adopted in three cantons of Switzerland, that little land of freedom which leads the world in popular government. The reform consists, briefly, in abolishing the district and ward system of electing single representatives, and then electing all the representatives on a general ticket as our presidential electors are elected. But instead of giving all the candidates to the majority party, as we do with presidential electors, the successful candidates are assigned to all parties in the field in nearly exact proportion to the popular vote of those parties. Thus, in a municipal election for aldermen, if fifty are to be elected, a group of reformers numbering only one-fiftieth of the total number of voters can join together, though they may be scattered in all parts of the city, can nominate the ablest man among themselves and can be absolutely sure of his election. If they number five-fiftieths they can elect five aldermen, and so on. Every group of reformers would likewise secure its fair proportion of representatives.

I cannot now enter into a full discussion of proportional representation.[1] Suffice it to say

[1] See Sir John Lubbock, " Representation," Imperial Parliament Series; " La Représentation Proportionnelle," Paris, 1888. Also *Proportional Representation Review*, Stoughton Cooley, secretary and editor, 22 Fifth Avenue, Chicago, Ill.

that in a highly complex political structure like ours the *method* whereby you work is fully as important as the *zeal* with which you work. In more primitive conditions great reforms might be introduced by a Charlemagne or a Napoleon by mere decree and force of arms. But in a civilization based on popular rule an avenue must be provided whereby reforms can gradually work up from the ranks of the people. Else revolution and reaction ensue.

Consider how far a legislature constituted as I have proposed agrees with an ideal assembly, and what such an assembly could accomplish for reform. A legislative assembly as a whole should not be more advanced than the people as a whole. A legislature made up altogether of reformers would be ludicrous and short-lived. But all shades of opinion, and all varieties of purpose, among the people at large should be accurately represented as soon as they attain political significance. In this way those who are united on a definite program should secure representation in proportion to their numbers. For this reason the constitution of the legislature should be elastic and readily responsive to the growth of popular sentiment. At present, as is well known, reform elements do not get representation until they have almost a majority of the people, and are on the verge of complete ascendency. Again, the legislature should be composed not of the average intelligence of the community, but of the leaders of the people. If democracy means rule by mediocrity, then democracy must fail. The ability of the community will somehow find means for ruling. It is the mediocrity rather than the corruption of our legislatures to-day that guarantees the supremacy of the machine and the lobby. Lastly, the representative leaders of the people should be secure in their seats so long as they truly represent a political fraction of the people. Machine methods, gerrymanders, distribution of spoils, should not be permitted to exclude them as soon as they have gained a little experience in legislation. From one-half to two-thirds of our law-makers to-day are not re-elected, and it is a rare thing to find a member of a State legislature who has served

more than three short terms. Truly this is
the secret of legislative incapacity and dull con-
servatism. Reform is experiment. Inexperi-
enced men do not venture far from the beaten
path. They follow the narrow footsteps of
their predecessors.

What now could be accomplished for social
reform and the Christianizing of society by a
legislature thus constituted ? Let us take the
case of a city council. It would be composed
of the ablest men in the city, representing all
interests and opinions. They would mainly be
men of experience in municipal affairs, and
would feel that they had a life-career before
them. Being independent of the sinister influences of the machine and the lobby, they
would devote themselves, not to distributing
spoils and favoring private monopolies, but
would study carefully the exigencies of municipal affairs. They would become well grounded
in the principles of economics and sociology.
The baser and corrupt elements of the city
would indeed be also represented. Gamblers
and saloon-keepers would send their leaders to

the council; but instead of getting a majority of the aldermen, as to-day, they would get only as many as were proportional to their numbers. And there is not a city in the land, not even the worst, where the baser elements on a fair count are not far in the minority.

A council thus composed would be a deliberative assembly. It would be the leaders of the people in conference. Let the tenement-house question, for example, come before them. Besides the three or four men, perhaps, who were the recognized leaders of this reform in the city, there would be a majority of the council well disposed. The larger number would be well informed as to what other cities in America and Europe were doing to meet this momentous problem. At present, if the people of a city want the tenement districts improved, they are compelled to form a voluntary society, to get up petitions, to go before a council wholly ignorant and even ill-disposed, and almost inevitably to accomplish nothing permanent unless they can strangely command some political influence. But with a properly constituted council, the leaders of the reform would have seats in the council. They could compel a hearing. Around them the outside sentiment of the city would concentrate. They would speak with authority. Their plans would indeed be thoroughly scrutinized and perhaps modified by the combined wisdom of all, but in some form or other they would command assent. Thus the reform would have a recognized nucleus. Reformers would find encouragement in their work. Instead of a helpless band of private dreamers, they would be a weighty, growing influence in the city. The reform itself would progress as rapidly as public education prepared the people for it, instead of being blocked by an indifferent, ignorant, and corrupt board of aldermen.

The same is true of every other reform. Street-cleaning, sewerage, local monopolies, public works, saloons, would all be dealt with in a scientific, progressive fashion. The municipal council, instead of being an obstacle to municipal reform, would be the wise and experienced leader. Good men would seek places in its deliberations, knowing that thereby they could exert a potent influence in bettering the conditions of their fellow-citizens. Applied Christianity could find its true place in municipal reform instead of being ignominiously excluded. And when the same principles should be extended to State legislatures and the federal Congress we must surely agree that for the first time the key to the social situation would be held, and that by far the most important practical advance would be made towards realizing on earth the kingdom of God.

Another legislative reform, which is to-day perhaps nearer adoption than proportional representation, is the so-called direct legislation of the Swiss cantons and federation. This takes two forms, the initiative and the referendum. By the initiative a specified number of private citizens may draw up a bill for enactment and present it to the legislature. The legislature cannot modify the bill, but must set a day on which the people are to vote for or against it as presented, just as we vote on con-

stitutional amendments. The referendum, as
its name indicates, is the constitutional pro-
vision that no act originating in and passed by
a legislature shall be valid as law unless the
people give a majority vote in its favor at the
polls.[1]

Direct legislation would be a powerful instrument for progressive reform in the present
political exigencies. It would largely remove
reform questions from party politics, and permit the people to vote their real sentiments
on important measures. By it many questions
which are now pressing, but which cannot get
a hearing in legislatures, would be immediately
settled.

But direct legislation alone cannot carry
social reform beyond a limited field. It is at
best only a powerful check on the legislature.
It gives little opportunity for deliberation and
compromise in the shaping of measures, which
is the essence of legislation and politics. It

[1] See J. W. Sullivan, "Direct Legislation," New York,
1893. Also address E. H. Pratt, Secretary Direct Legislation
League, P. O. Box 1216, New York.

does not provide for experienced, able, and honest leaders in framing laws. The people in voting cannot take into account the details of bills, and in a complex civilization the details of legislation are vital. Consequently, as is found to be the case in Switzerland, the people do not vote upon the merits of measures, but upon the question of "confidence" or "no confidence" in the legislature which proposes them. Thereby much progressive legislation is defeated. Two-thirds of the laws submitted are vetoed by the people, and many of them afterward in the same form are eagerly adopted. But direct legislation combined with proportional representation seems, as already shown, to be exactly fitted to the needs of the political situation.

Two other reforms in the machinery of government are necessary before politics can take its place in a programme of social reform. They are the secret ballot and civil service reform. These are fully as important as those I have described, but are much better known and are rapidly on the road to adoption.

The question, what should be the attitude of the Church toward politics, is already inferred if not answered. But in conclusion let me emphasize it. In the times of our ancestors the Church and the State were one. Ecclesiastical questions were political questions. The two were deliberated and decided in the same assembly. To-day we have wisely separated Church and State. But we have carried it too far. We have separated Christians and politics. Christians are here to save the world, that is, to reform the world. They must begin by reforming politics. They must reform both the machinery and the spirit of politics, the structure and the functions of government. Political reform is not an end in itself. It is a means for attaining fundamental social reforms. It is the doorway to the practical solution of the problems of labor, taxation, crime, pauperism ; and these are but the Christian problems, how to save the world, and how to save every individual in the world. First, the people must study these social questions. There is no force in society so able to give them the right direction in their study as the spirit of Christianity. And having found what is wanted, the next thing is to find how to get it. Legislative reform in the shape of proportional representation and direct legislation is indispensable to facilitate both. These reforms would educate the people as no other institution could do, and would furnish the unfailing machinery for enforcing the plans which education has led the people to adopt. So important are these as a key to all social reforms, that with their adoption we might expect greater social progress in five years than the present bungling methods permit in twenty-five years.

TEMPERANCE REFORM.

TEMPERANCE REFORM.[1]

INTEMPERANCE is a social problem. To cure it this fact must be recognized. Morselli has said that suicide, insanity, crime, vagabondage, are phenomena of civilization. So is intemperance. Ours has been a century of revolution. Old forms of social organization have been suddenly demolished. Customs and laws which regulated the lives of men have been repealed or disregarded. Every man has been left to his fate or his fortune without any recognized guidance. It has been an age of scramble. In the melee those unable to scramble have gone to the bottom.

Man differs from other animals mainly in his nervous system. This is the seat of his feel-

[1] REFERENCES: Norman M. Kerr, "Inebriety," London, 1888; T. L. Wright, M. D., "Inebriism," Bellefontaine, O.; *Quarterly Journal of Inebriety*, Hartford, Conn.

ings, his intelligence, his will. In his struggle for existence the brute depends upon his teeth, his claws, his muscle. Civilized man depends upon his nerves and his brain. It is with these that he adjusts himself to his surroundings. It is his nervous system that makes him a social animal. When adjustment with society fails, it is upon his nervous system that the greatest strain occurs. This system is most delicately balanced. It is easily weakened or upset. Society is in a state of convulsion. Maladjustment with such a society is inevitable. The individual is then on the verge of that nervous degeneracy which the psychologists ascribe to the abnormal man.

This maladjustment has shown itself in startling figures the past forty years. During that time crime has increased five times as fast as population. Insanity has doubled and trebled compared with population. Suicide has increased alarmingly. Paupers have multiplied, and tramp is a new word, while intemperance has become so fixed and ascertainable that it is known as inebriety. The consumption of alcoholic liquors per capita of the nation at large has more than doubled in twenty years, notwithstanding that the proportion of total abstainers has largely increased. Those who drink are more excessive than ever before ; and the proportion of drunkards has also increased.

What can be done to check this flood of evil ? What can the Church do ? To answer these questions we must first know the nature and the causes of inebriety. When science has taught us these, Christianity and science may point out the remedies.

From the standpoint of the nervous system, then, what is intemperance ? It is the excessive use of some anæsthetic, either alcohol, opium, chloral, chloroform, ether, or chlorodyne. The craving of the drunkard for this anæsthetic is not owing to any pleasant taste in the mouth. It is an overwhelming demand of the entire nervous system. In other words, inebriety is allied to insanity and epilepsy on the one hand, and hay fever on the other. An unbalanced nervous system, having its origin in many different causes, gives rise to the most intense feelings of unrest, irritability, and a peculiar nagging sensation, as though the whole body were in a state of terrible unceasing agitation. These feelings, accompanied by the memory derived from previous experience on the part of the sufferer, that alcohol or some other anæsthetic will quiet the nerves, creates the irresistible craving for that anæsthetic. It is a morbid appetite; but it is overwhelming, and is far more inexorable than the simple appetite of taste for some palatable drink. The drunkard loathes the taste of whiskey. He washes it out of his mouth with a glass of water. It is not the *intoxicant* he wants, but the *intoxication.*

The fact that most inebriety among Tuetonic peoples is *alcoholic*, is an historical accident. The diseased condition of the nervous system is the essential fact. With us it takes the form of alcoholism. With Asiatics it is opium-eating. It may be also chloral, chlorodyne, or ether. But alcohol has an advantage over other anæsthetics in that it is also a stimulant. Its first action is to spur the circulation. It exhilarates and then soothes.

Inebriety, being a disease of the nervous system, should be studied by the physiologist and the physician. The question to be answered is, what is the nature of the structural degeneration of nerve walls and nerve cells which causes these feelings of nervous agony? The medical writers hold that the disease may be very different in character for different persons. In one it may be an excessive growth of the nerves and nerve cells, hypertrophy; in another a defective nutrition, atrophy; in another an unequal development, especially where the brain has been cultivated at the expense of the nerves. In some it may be the unnatural growth and hardening of the walls of the nerve cells, thus crowding upon the nerve matter itself. Or, there may be a fatty degeneration of the nerve substance. And finally it may be a constitutional blood-poisoning which has eaten away parts of the nerves. In all cases there is some structural defect in the substance of the nerves or brain. And this is exactly the case in insanity.

The close relation between insanity and inebriety is a potent revelation from the scientific students of intemperance. I do not refer to the fact that a drunken man acts and talks like an insane man, for the shallowest student can see that; but to the fact that the *causes* which lead him to drink are similar to those which impel the insane man to his mad acts. The inebriate is insane while he is sober.

Dr. T. L. Wright[1] speaks of three kinds of alcoholic inebriates. First, the daily, habitual drunkard, who is popularly believed to drink "simply from motives of baseness, idleness, and reckless diabolism. He is supposed to be wholly in love and accord with evil from choice."

Second, the moderate drinker, who does not get intoxicated. This man is blamed mainly because of his bad example, and not because of any direct injury to himself or others. "Yet," says Dr. Wright, "it will appear in the sequel that this steady drinker is the unwitting father not only of a dreadful fate to himself, but that from him, especially, through organic nerve changes which eventually become hereditary,

[1] "Inebriism," page 34.

spring not the inebriate and the lunatic alone, but not uncommonly the criminal also."

Third, the periodic or spasmodic drunkard, the man who reforms, signs the pledge, shows deep remorse, and then plunges headlong into the wildest excess of intoxication, again to reform and repeat the same cycle. "He is," says Dr. Wright, "a standing puzzle, . . . the source of more hopes and more fears, more suspense and dread, more admiration and disgust, than any other species of drunkard." He is the true type of the drunkard in his essential nature, and in his make-up will be found the various causes of inebriety.

The causes of inebriety, like those of other diseases, may be fruitfully classed as predisposing and exciting. Predisposing causes are "those which render the body susceptible to disease; exciting causes are those which excite an outbreak of the disease in bodies previously predisposed to it."[1] We may examine the different causes of inebriety from these standpoints.

[1] Kerr, "Inebriety," page 134.

Of course, the most patent cause of inebriety is alcohol itself. Alcohol is a poison. Its daily moderate use results in abnormal growth and hardening of the connective tissues and cell walls throughout the body, especially in the liver, kidneys, and brain. Plainly, as a result, the inner substance of these organs must be gradually compressed and strangled. The nerve matter is disturbed in its action and degenerates day by day. Finally the point is reached where the balance is upset, and, when an exciting cause is presented, the moderate drinker becomes the outrageous drunkard. The nervous system becomes disorganized and unstable, and nothing can quiet it except his familiar anæsthetic and stimulant.

But it is agreed by the highest authorities, that the use of intoxicants by a perfectly healthy person is only one of the minor causes of the disease inebriety. Says Dr. Wright, " The greater proportion of the oinomaniacal neuroses is to be found in those who have received them by inheritance, from the epilepsy, the insanity, the vices, and misfortunes, and physical injuries of a world long since dead and gone."

Alcohol as an exciting agent must of course always be present, else there could be no intoxication. Its seriousness occurs where a person already subject to nervous disease through predisposing causes, is induced to take the first glass of liquor. In such a person there follows an immediate frenzied seizure upon the intoxicant as soon as he perceives that it allays the nervous instability and agony which he suffers. The slightest smell of alcohol will re-awaken the old crave of the reformed drunkard, and his will is powerless before it. Children who have inherited the diseased or unstable condition often show a wild yearning for an intoxicant which once they have tasted.

Here is, of course, the supreme argument for the prohibition of the liquor traffic. Children and young people must not be allowed the first taste of liquor, and the exciting agent must be removed from the reforming drunkard.

To physical and mental shocks are ascribed by Dr. Crothers twenty per cent of all inebriety. These are especially "blows on the head, sunstrokes, railroad accidents, and injuries which have caused stupor or periods of unconsciousness, or profound wasting diseases." [1] The mental shocks are domestic, business and financial trouble, religious hysteria, disappointed affections, and fright.[2]

Other diseases which lead to inebriety are those affecting the vital organs and the blood, such as lung disease, dyspepsia, licentiousness, rheumatism, and gout. Shocks and diseases result in abnormal nutrition or degeneracy of the nerves and brain, thus calling for narcotic relief.

Diet, sanitary conditions, and occupation, combined with heredity, are the most far-reaching of the predisposing causes of intemperance. The diet of the rich may be too luxurious, that of the poor unwholesome, insufficient, and innutritious. The nervous system is not sufficiently nourished, and there is a craving for something to stimulate and soothe. The salted meats and the adulterated

[1] *North American Review*, Sept., 1891.   [2] Kerr, page 181.

groceries of the poor, together with their ignorance of cooking, are probably a co-operating cause for more than half our intemperance. Children are brought up without wholesome or sufficient food, their bodies are starved and puny, and when they grow older and are compelled to work, their strength cannot withstand the nervous strain. Intoxicating drink is their inevitable refuge. I know of no temperance reform more urgently needed than cooking schools.

Bad diet is usually found with bad homes. Says Dr. Kerr : " Ill-ventilated and overcrowded dwellings, from the vitiated state of the air within them, occasion a languor and sluggishness which lead to functional derangement, and produce a profound feeling of depression which, in many cases, predisposes and excites to intemperance in alcohol." Tenement-house reform is profound temperance reform.

Occupation underlies many other causes. It determines diet and tenement. In itself it acts in two ways. In the learned professions and business enterprises, where there is usually a sensitive nervous organism combined with modern high-pressure competition, nervous irritability arouses the craving for intoxicants. Stock-brokers, editors, physicians, are especially liable.

But these classes usually have *variety* in their work. Competition with variety often strengthens the mind and nerves. In our insane asylums the largest proportion of inmates is furnished from farmers' wives. It is high pressure combined with *monotony* that causes insanity. So with intemperance. The working classes of our day do not learn an all-around trade. They are appendages to machines. Their occupation is cramped; they work in a groove; the intellect is not invited. Long hours, heated and unsanitary surroundings, and no variety in their work, lead to a craving for stimulant and anæsthetic.

Heredity is wholly predisposing. Dr. Crothers ascribes to it sixty per cent of intemperance. Here we see the close relation between inebriety and insanity. A notable fact of heredity is the interchangeability of nervous diseases. Heredity does not necessarily produce *identity*, it produces *like*. Dr. Kerr[1] says of the off-spring of insane parentage, that one child may be an idiot, a second an epileptic, a third becomes insane at puberty, a fourth is an inebriate, and a fifth is neuralgic. And so with the families of many inebriates. One member is insane, a second is hysteric, a third is melancholic, a fourth is asthmatic, a fifth is an inebriate.

But it is not necessary that parents be insane or inebriate in order to beget a predisposition to intemperance in their children. Consumption, rheumatism, gout, or some profound constitutional disease, will do the same. The overwork of mothers in factories and sweatshops is the very hothouse of drunkenness for generations to come. Whatever bequeathes a defective or deficient nervous system will predispose the inheritor to inebriety.[2]

---

[1] "Inebriety," page 29.

[2] Whatever may be the outcome of the present discussion on the question, "Are acquired characters inherited?" it seems

To these four causes, bad diet, bad homes, occupation, and heredity, co-operating and cumulative, may safely be attributed three-fourths of our modern intemperance.

Other causes might be mentioned. The voluntary idleness of the rich and the tramp, the involuntary idleness of the honest workingman. In modern industry long hours of exhausting work alternate with seasons of out-of-work. Intemperance in drinking is the corollary of intemperance in working.

Our system, too, of popular education, by putting undue strain on the intellect at the expense of the body, and establishing an arbitrary exalted standard which only the brilliant can attain, results in nerve irritability, and sows the seeds of intemperance.

With this survey of the causes of intemper-

probable that the above conclusions will not be overthrown. For, should the question be decided negatively, it would apply only to those characters acquired through use and disuse, while profound constitutional degeneration, affecting the vital organs and the blood of the parent, could by no possibility bequeath a healthy body to the offspring. To inherit inebriety is not to inherit a mouth-taste for liquor, but it is to inherit a debilitated constitution and defective nerves.

ance before us, it is plain that no single panacea will effect its cure. The disease is as deep as civilization. The cure is the whole range of social reform. Let us rapidly survey these reforms. The first to notice are those measures which *prevent* the origin of an unstable nervous condition. A healthy body and a healthy nervous system are the first requisites. The diet can be improved by plain instead of luxurious living on the part of the rich, especially for children, by cooking schools along with common and high schools for rich and poor, and by laws against the adulteration of food.

Tenement-house reform involves more than inspection. It involves demolition, and it may involve municipal ownership and management, as in Liverpool and Glasgow. Certainly it depends on cheaper street-car fares, and these can be adequately secured only through municipal ownership of lines. Sanitation in dwellings and factories will cure intemperance as it lowers the death rate.

The level of competition in business must be

raised. Competition is good ; but excessive, prolonged competition is degrading. Here government must intervene. There are needed shorter hours of labor, protection from Sunday labor, Saturday half-holidays, factory laws protecting women and children, and abolition of sweat-shops.

Wages, too, must be better, especially for the lowest laborers, and there must be security of employment and better educational methods.

When all these social reforms are carried out, it will be possible to have universal prohibition. This is a preventive measure, but not a positive cure. It should be extended wherever it can be enforced. Sweden and Norway and South Carolina have shown us the next best system. They have taken the element of *private profit* out of the retail liquor business, and have made it a government monopoly. They have substituted *public profit*. There is danger that this, in relieving the people from taxes, may operate against further prohibition; but at any rate it is better than

our system of high license, which combines
the twin evils of private profit and public
profit. It seems plain, however, that intoxicating liquors ought not to be sold at cost.
The profits must then be enormous. Norway
has hit upon the plan of turning them in to
various charitable, religious, and reformatory
institutions. This is the best that can be
done, but it looks like a bonus to the saviours
of society not to oppose the industry that
gives them something to do.

So much for the prevention of drunkenness.
Can the drunkard himself be cured? At present there are two cures that have the approval
of the public, moral suasion and imprisonment.
Both are sad failures. Notwithstanding the
influences of religion and moral suasion, and
the periodic cycles of temperance revival, the
per capita consumption of liquor has doubled
in twenty years.

Imprisonment, on the other hand, is not
only not a cure, it is a powerful stimulus to
the disease. It is said that ninety-nine per
cent of the drunkards who are committed to

prison are sure to appear again for the same offence.   One woman in England has been committed two hundred and fifty times for drunkenness, and American workhouses have " rounders " whose records run from twenty to one hundred and fifty commitments.   This is indeed the climax of that burlesque which we fondly call "justice."   We simply clean up the drunkard for fifteen to thirty days, then send him out with a pungent, newly whetted appetite for another debauch.

When inebriety is recognized as a disease, the chains of morality will not be broken, as many fear, nor will the drunkard be petted and fed with honey, but he will be treated like a madman.   Industrial hospitals will take the place of workhouses in the vicinity of large towns and cities, for temporary cases, and there will be one or more State hospitals for their permanent treatment.   Admission will be voluntary or compulsory.   Treatment will be scientific, military, medical, and hygienic.   The inmate will be compelled to work, he will be taught a trade, his surplus earnings will be set apart for his family and dependents or for himself on release. He will not be sent up for thirty days, but *until cured.* Succeeding commitments will be cumulative, and the third or fourth will prove him incurable. He will then be confined for life. When in the judgment of the physician and superintendent he is cured he will be released not unconditionally, but *on parole,* with official supervision and monthly reports, to be returned, if he backslides, on a warrant from the superintendent without the intervention of the courts.

This is the best that medical science and prison science together offer for the cure of drunkenness. But all positive cures have organic relations with preventive measures. The disease is curable, or at least its course can be checked, but there are two indispensable conditions : *total abstinence,* and *freedom from predisposing and exciting causes.* The first condition involves prohibition, the second involves social reform. As long as men are overworked, involuntarily idle, have poor food and bad homes, there is no permanent cure for their drunkenness.

I have not spoken directly of the place of the Church in this matter of intemperance. Yet everything I have said is directly the true work of the Church. There is, however, one profound fact and one unbounded field of work which I have omitted. Human conduct is fundamentally a movement away from pain. A man drinks because it gives him pleasure and relieves his pain. If he does not drink, it is because he finds greater pleasure elsewhere. But man differs from the brute in this: His pleasures may be those of art, literature, politics, religion, benevolence. These are refined and exquisite. They leave no room for drunkenness. The whole thing is a question of what we call character. The highest character finds happiness in these highest activities; the lowest, only in sensual indulgence. To merely tell a man to quit drinking is mockery. Tell him to quit, and then build up his character so that he can have pleasure in better things. Here is the work of the Church — the old work of character-building, but on a broader basis than ever before. It is not merely conventional worship, but everything that gives the man a better body, a better nervous system, a broader outlook. It is the institutional church in its fullest scope. It is the friendly visitors, organized, intelligent, faithful. I have advocated shorter hours and better wages as essential temperance reform. Yet I know these cannot be safely granted to men whose minds are low. It is the duty of the Church to make men worthy of industrial and social reform. Individual reform must accompany social reform. Each is essential to the other. Intemperance is a social disease and an individual disease. It must be attacked from both sides. Christianity and true religion are equal to the attack if only they summon to their aid psychology and sociology.

MUNICIPAL MONOPOLIES.

MUNICIPAL MONOPOLIES.

MODERN society is marked by three momentous but quiet revolutions, which distinguish it from any that have preceded. The first is a moral, the second a technical, the third an economic revolution.

The moral revolution is that remarkable humanitarian wave which is showing itself in religion, politics, industry. The Sunday-school scholar of to-day knows almost nothing of the creeds and catechisms which engrossed the childhood of our mothers ; but he learns about the Man Christ, and scarcely gets a hint at the wrath and vengeance of God. The politician protests by the heavens above and the earth beneath that he is above all the friend of the workingman. In industry the air is rife with schemes for profit-sharing, co-operation, and socialism.

All this is a new way of looking at things.
The world has shifted its moral standpoint. A
revolution has occurred in the very hearts of
men. And a moral revolution is the all-important one in society. It is the beliefs, the hopes,
the ideals of men that transform and renovate
their social institutions. Everything else must
conform to these new ideas. The standpoint
which we shall take to-day on every social and
industrial question is determined mainly by the
way we look at this revolution in morals.

The technical revolution consists in the un-
paralleled march of science and invention. Nature is made the slave of man instead of his
master. The locomotive engineer is as mighty
as ten thousand Greeks and Romans. This
technical revolution effects its greatest results
in the means of communication and transportation. It has separated the farmer from the
manufacturer by thousands of miles. It has
built up cities like condensed empires. It has
caused a minute and rigid division of labor.
And this, more important than all else, has
made men dependent upon each other for their

very livelihood. No one nowadays supplies all his own wants. He performs one little service for society at large, and looks to society for his own sustenance. Hence, those industries which are called distributive are the most vital of all. They furnish the only avenues for carrying the products of the individual out to society, distributing them among his fellowmen, and, in turn, of bringing back to the individual the products which society has made for him. The individual cannot do this. He must rely upon social servants to do it. If I be dependent upon you for my life, much more am I dependent upon the means of communication for reaching you. These industries we rightly look upon as *public* services. They must have special favors from society, and society cannot withhold these because its life depends upon the services. Hence society grants them franchises, rights of way, the use of public highways, the sovereign powers of eminent domain. From the nature of the case it makes them monopolies. Competition, which presses down on other enterprises, is here unknown.

City monopolies are a special kind of these general distributive industries. But they are as vital to the city life as are railways and postal service to the nation. Cities cover to-day such wide areas, individuals have their industry so much more minutely divided than in the country, access to the free gifts of nature — like water, sunlight, fresh air — is necessarily so denied, competition is so relentless, that the city dweller must look to public servants for necessities which the countryman readily provides for himself.

The economic revolution is the rise and growth of private corporations. Unquestionably the corporations have made possible the present marvellous development of industry. They have opened up the resources of the country on a large scale, have conducted costly experiments, and brought about unnumbered economies. But private corporations in control of the distributive industries of a city are very different from the original experimental corporations. An argument was formerly in vogue to the effect that private business was always better managed than public, because the proprietor had a personal, immediate interest in the success of his business. He gave his individual attention to its oversight. He watched the details, took advantage of improvements, sought eagerly to please his customers and to solicit trade. These arguments held true regarding corporations, because the owners were always the originators and managers of their own business. But for city monopolies this is no longer true. These industries have passed far beyond the experimental stage. They supply necessities. They need none of the costly devices of advertising and bill-posting. Their market is constant. In good times or bad the people must patronize them. They are the safest kind of business that can possibly be entered upon. In this regard they even surpass distributive industries in the country at large, like railways and the telegraph. Cities are growing rapidly in size; no competitors can contend with these municipal monopolies for their growing market; and every increase in sales is accompanied by a diminishing cost

of production. Whether the business is man
aged well or ill, profits must swiftly increase.

Consequently we find as we should expect, a
change in the character of corporations owning
these enterprises. The stockholders are no
longer as a rule the managers. They have sur-
rendered their earlier functions into the hands
of salaried presidents, superintendents, and
attorneys. These are the men who really control such enterprises and deal with the customers. They are agents. The stockholders are
perhaps absentees. They look only for dividends. Their agents are responsible for the
dividends, not directly for the public services
they render.

With these facts recognized, the conclusion
is necessary that these industries must either
be controlled or owned by the city. Nobody
any longer favors leaving them alone. The
moral revolution has gone too far. These enterprises hold the dearest interests of the masses
in their hands. They employ thousands of
laborers. And, notwithstanding the city gives
to them the most valuable of special privileges,

there are no employers in the land who work their men so long or pay them so poorly, unless public control forces them into better ways. Besides, their charges are nearly always disproportionately far above the cost of their services, as measured by those of other industries. Every city in the land is in a constant fever of complaint because of the high charges and shabby services of these favored monopolies. The working girl, receiving only six dollars a week, is forced to stand morning and evening in a cold and crowded street car and deliver to the agents of the company at least one-tenth of her income. She is thus taxed in a relentless way that the government itself dare not attempt. The Manhattan Elevated of New York carries its passengers at the cost of two and one-half cents apiece and charges them five cents for doing it. This is simply the highway robbery of the poor. Gas and electric light are furnished at a prohibitory tariff.

But there is a corporation which is responsive to the demands of morals. This is the city itself. Private financiering is carried on for dividends. Public financiering is conducted for the good of the public. The moral revolution has passed by the private corporation, and is fast giving us a new goal for the municipal corporation.

There is a wide-spread complaint about the corruption of city government. Fault is found with the army of ignorant and boss-led voters. But how can a city government be pure and noble, when we look upon its reform merely as a matter of reducing the tax rate? Men are better than taxes. We shall never have upright city government until cities are regarded as means for elevating, widening, and rejoicing the life of the day-laborer, his wife and children. If the city does nothing for your ignorant voter, why should he not get something else for his vote? Let the city renovate the tenement house, even build its own tenement houses, as Liverpool and Glasgow have done ; let it regulate and inspect the markets, keep down extortion and pawnbroker's usury, as Berlin has done ; let it furnish cheap transportation and carry the children free to school and back, as Sydney and Melbourne have done ; let it furnish cheap gas, electric light and power, pure water, and even steam heat at cost to all the poorest, as various cities abroad and at home have done ; then should we have a city worth spending enthusiasm upon. Then would city government take hold of the hearts of the meanest voters. At present the workingman has nothing at stake in his municipality. He is a mere pack-horse, with a precarious shelter-at-will in somebody else's tenement. The city does nothing for him. What interest can he take in it ?

You may say this is not business — it is sentiment. Yes, it is sentiment. But he who counts upon ruling out the ethical impulses from politics, religion, or business, is revolting against the one social force that is resistless.

With this new view of city government arising in the hearts of men, economists are compelled to add new emphasis to the distinction between industries that are public, and those that are private. The distributive industries are public. We are only beginning to see how significant they are for the welfare of every other enterprise in the city. They must be made servants to them.

What, then, can public control and regulation short of ownership and management do, to make them fulfil their proper purpose? Massachusetts has established a State Board of Gas and Electric Light Commissioners with extraordinary powers. Upon complaint from any city, the board can make examination, and can order the company to charge reasonable rates and to establish reasonable conditions. Its decisions are final. The board has been in existence for eight years; yet in no State in the Union to-day is the demand for public ownership more urgent. Charges have been reduced in but a few cases through the efforts of the board, and then very insignificantly. The companies continue to pay high dividends on inflated stock, and the service, though somewhat improved, is far below that where cities own their plants. The commission protects the companies even more than the public. In many States the companies are advocating commissions to stem the tide for public ownership.

It is one thing to show what ought to be done, and another to show that it can be done. Can cities safely undertake these enterprises? Would not expenses be greater? Would not improvements cease to be added? Would not political corruption be increased?

There are four characteristics belonging to these enterprises, as compared with strictly private business, which render them peculiarly fit for public ownership and management.

In the first place, they are not experiments. They supply necessities. Unless the city itself withers away, they are sure to grow more profitable. Government in none of its forms can afford to take risks. If an individual fail in an experiment, he alone goes into bankruptcy. But if a government fail, bankruptcy means the beginning of anarchy. Government must be cautious, but cities run no risks whatever in these industries.

These enterprises, too, are monopolies. Government cannot safely engage in competition with private corporations. If government did not forbid private persons to carry the mails, the public post-office would prove a failure. This does not mean that public service is inefficient, but that public financiering is based on different principles from private. Its purpose is the development of the country, of the city, the encouragement of industry, the equalizing of conditions, the welfare of the masses. A private post-office would give magnificent service between the great cities and wealthy patrons. It would carry letters in cities for half a cent. But the South and West, the poor and the isolated, would have no service whatever, or else would pay extortionate prices. The Atlantic coast and Great Lake regions support the post-office, and pay for all the country. Other sections are served at heavy loss. This can be done only by enforcing a monopoly or by imposing taxes. So it is with a municipal enterprise. Like the streets and highways, it is a necessary condition and stimulus for private business. It ought not to be conducted for profit, but for service. For effecting this result it must be a monopoly.

Again, these enterprises are pre-eminently simple in their organization. There are no complex, minute details. There is little delicacy of adjustment. Not a great amount of skill is required from the workmen. A large number of employees perform the same operation. They can be organized like an army. The accounts are easily kept, and the public can understand them.

And lastly, the workmen are constantly under the eye of their employers, the public. The public is capable of judging as to the quality of the service. Complaint is easily made. The manager and superintendents are your neighbors. If they are responsible to you they will serve you well.

These are four advantages which render it presumptive that city governments could successfully own and operate these enterprises. Experience, also, as far as it can be gathered, realizes these presumptions. City ownership and management, in every known case where

it has been tried, is superior to private ownership and management.   I can stop here only to
give final results and averages, as far as these
enterprises have been studied, and refer you
for details to other sources.[1]

According to the census report of 1892, the
average annual charge for water for an average
dwelling in thirty-six cities owning their works,
was $11.50 for an average daily per capita con-
sumption of ninety gallons ; while in fourteen
cities under private ownership, the charge was
$17.42, or an average of fifty-one per cent
higher.   The lowest charge was for public
ownership, $4.50.   The highest was for private

[1] Statistical data following are derived from the "Census
Bulletins" of 1890; "Consular Report on Gas in Foreign
Countries; " *Review of Reviews*, February, 1893, articles on
Municipal Gas-making and Electric Lighting in the United
States; *The Aegis*, Madison, Wisconsin, containing report of
a debate on Municipal Ownership; Bemis, " Public Ownership
of Gas in the United States," in publications of the American
Economic Association.   The statistics are ably criticised, how-
ever, by Rosewater in publications of the American Statistical
Association, 1893, volume iii., Numbers 21 and 22.   Mr.
Rosewater apparently does not deny the conclusions to be
drawn from the statistics, since he advocates municipal ownership.   He rightly enjoins caution in the use of the figures,
especially in the matter of averages.

ownership, $31.00. The average cost of the works under city ownership was $21.35 to each head of population, while, under private owner-ship, companies were paying dividends on $31.20 per capita, being forty-six per cent higher.

In the manufacture of gas, European cities have gone ahead of American cities. In Ger-many, fifty per cent of the cities own their works, and the charges are, in every case, less than for private services. Berlin clears $1,200,000 a year on her municipal gas, and sells it for $1.00 a thousand. New York, with the same population, pays $1.25 a thousand, and gets nothing but a small lot of taxes and a big lot of bribed aldermen.

In England, public works have increased in sixteen years twenty-three per cent, while private works have increased 19 88 per cent. The average price charged by public works is 2s. 6d. — sixty cents — the average by private works is 2s. 9½d. — sixty-seven cents. It is a gen-eral fact that with public ownership the con-sumption of gas and other services is much smaller in proportion to the number of con-

sumers than with private ownership, showing
that the public serves the poorer classes.   In
England, it stands twenty-nine thousand feet
per consumer in public works, and fifty-five
thousand in private ; while with public works
the number of consumers is fifteen per cent of
the population, and with private works it is only
eight and one-half per cent.

In the United States there are but twelve
cities owning gas-works.   Two of these secured their works in 1892 and one in 1891.
Philadelphia, notwithstanding a worn-out plant
and wide areas, manufactures and delivers gas
for seventy-six cents per thousand feet ; and,
making allowance for extensions, interest, and
taxes, the cost would be $1.06.   She sells it
for $1.50, clears over $1,000,000 a year, and
with her water-works reduces the tax-rate on
other property sixty cents on the hundred dollars.

The city of Wheeling, with thirty-five thousand population, made and delivered gas in 1892
for fifty-seven cents per thousand feet, allowing
seven per cent for interest and taxes ; sold the

gas for seventy-five cents to private consumers, furnished free all gas used by the city, and cleared twenty-eight thousand dollars cash.

The average cost for nine cities which have been in the business for more than two years is sixty-four cents a thousand. The cost of making gas is rapidly falling. Water gas can be made and sold for thirty-five cents. If a city owns its works, it gets the advantage of such improvements. Otherwise no reductions are made. Philadelphia, having her own pipes, buys water gas in the holders for thirty-seven cents.

The number of consumers in Philadelphia is thirteen per cent of the population. In Wheeling ten per cent. In Boston, with private ownership, it is only seven per cent.

Public works can be duplicated in cities of twenty thousand population and over at a cost of about three dollars per thousand feet of product. As cities can borrow for four per cent, the allowance for interest would be about twelve cents per thousand. In twenty-two large cities the companies are paying handsome dividends on a capitalization of $7.72 per thousand feet. If dividends are six per cent, this would be an average monopoly squeezing of forty-six cents on the thousand feet. In Chicago, with a capitalization of $10.63, it would be sixty cents a thousand.

Electric lighting shows even more startling comparisons. The average cost per light per year of arcs operated by twenty-three cities is $53.04. Making the very liberal allowance of twelve per cent on the total cost of plant and buildings, for interest, depreciation, and taxes, the average cost is $86.64, and, at an allowance of seven per cent the cost is only $75.64. But twenty-nine private companies under substantially similar conditions, and for the same lights, receive an average of $106.61 — from twenty to forty per cent higher than public cost.

There are very few cities, abroad or at home, which own and operate their street railways. But Plymouth, Glasgow, and London have recently purchased portions of their lines and have just begun to operate them. Thirty-three English cities own their lines but lease them to companies. Toronto operated its lines for six months at a profit of twenty-five thousand dollars per month, but has leased them to a private company for twelve thousand dollars per month.

The enormous profits of street railway lines is well known, as well as the magnificent stock-watering which is based upon them. The Manhattan Elevated of New York City, costing $22,000,000, is bonded and stocked at $70,000,000, pays six per cent dividends, and its inflated stock sells at one hundred and seventy dollars. Nearly every city in the country shows these roads paying good dividends on from two to five times their cost.

Now, what could be done by cities if they owned and operated their railways? In the first place, they can borrow money at two-thirds the rate paid by private corporations. They would not seek profits, but could immediately reduce charges one-half. Traffic would be greatly increased. Private corporations are often short-sighted in the conduct of their own business. The State of Iowa through its State commission reduced the charges for railway freight in that state eighteen per cent. The railways protested, and had the law declared unconstitutional by the federal court. But they did not ask to have the judicial decree enforced, because, in the mean time, their net earnings had increased twenty-five per cent. Hungary reduced the passenger charges on her state railways seventy-five per cent, and the traffic increased nearly five hundred per cent, while the net earnings increased thirty to forty per cent.

Not only would cities lower the charges, they would also improve the service. The poorer districts would receive extensions, cars would be furnished in abundance, warm coaches would be substituted for hay-barns. Better wages would be paid, drivers protected from the cold, shorter hours and holidays would be provided.

What would be the effect upon the business industry of the city? Every family would save twenty to forty dollars from street-car fares to spend for clothing, groceries, shoes, and amusements. Profits from the street-car business would be spent at home instead of in Europe. This would increase the business of a city by hundreds of thousands of dollars. Laboring people could live in the country, and own their homes. They would take a personal interest in city government. Tenements would not be crowded. Sanitary conditions would be improved and the death-rate lowered. Men out of work could ride in search of employment, instead of wearily tramping the streets. Laborers would be in better health, have better food, do better work, and all city industries would be materially advanced and stimulated. So great are the possibilities of cheap transportation that I believe the time will come when cities will carry freight as well as passengers, and will perform this work free of charge, paying the expenses out of taxes. Consider what a blight it would be to have our streets themselves owned by private companies, and every pedestrian compelled to pay toll when going through the turnstile or under the gates. As cities grow in size and become overcrowded, the actual work of transportation will become as important, and will have to be done on the same principle, as the present work of merely paving, bridging, and cleaning the streets.

I need not go further to show what are the possibilities of city ownership and management. Everybody concedes most of this. But you are doubtless thinking, "All this is very fine, but do you not know that city government in America is the most corrupt thing on earth? You want to increase the civil service five or ten times. You want to put thousands of employees in the ranks of spoils. You want a carnival of corruption. You want to bring these important enterprises into politics."

Now, I ask, can they ever be deeper in politics than they are to-day? They, unlike other kinds of business, depend directly upon legislation for their franchises. And if we adopt more stringent public control, we but increase their dependence on politics. But, if they be owned by the city, to whose interest would it be to bribe aldermen and legislators? What would become of the lobby? Would aldermen and legislators introduce bills in order to blackmail them, and then withdraw the bills? In fact, city ownership takes them out of politics. This is universally the case in the cities of Europe; and even in our own corrupt cities, the same is true.

Yet I do not belittle this side of the question. I agree that city government must be improved before these industries can be safely intrusted to it. In the minds of nearly every one, this is the only stumbling block in the way of city operation. Therefore, here is where our most earnest attention must be directed.

The question is one simply of choosing agents. The only advantage now possessed by a private corporation over a municipal one, is the greater ability and freedom of private stockholders in selecting managers and operators. They do not attend to the management themselves. They choose others to do it. And this is what a city must do if it operates its own works.

The problem, then, is one of the civil service. Is it impossible to devise a system of public selection which shall choose able and experienced men to carry on public enterprises, which shall make them responsible to the people and not to the party managers, and which shall give them secure tenure of office so long as they do their work well? Private corporations do this. Can public corporations do the same?

I do not believe that America need fall behind Europe and Australia in this matter. They have perfect and incorruptible city governments. Cannot we?

It is not necessary to imitate foreign cities. Our problems are our own. They must be solved in our own way. And he is quite blind who does not see that we are beginning to solve them. First, we have about settled the question of the mayor. We have discovered the secret of individual personal responsibility. We have done nothing yet for councils and boards of aldermen, except to shear them of their power. But the time will soon come when they will be as well under control as the mayor. Why is it that American cities have capable, economical fire departments? It is be-

cause the insurance companies put up the pre-
miums, and the business community is forced,
through the nerves of its pocket-book, to bring
the fire department into line with upright business principles. The same can be done for
every other department of city government.
Let us take the fire department as a model.
Let us improve it in places. Let us apply its
methods to the entire city government. Then
there will be no question of political corruption.

I will sketch the way in which it seems to
me the thing can be done, taking as a model
certain features of the fire departments in
various cities of the Union.

Let us suppose that the city has purchased
the street-cars and purposes to operate them.
First, the mayor is the one responsible head
for the city government. He appoints a single
head of the department of transportation, who
is responsible to him and none other. This director of transportation is appointed only during the term of the mayor, and is therefore not
an operative or superintendent, but a political

officer, who determines the general policy of his department and represents it before the people.

The director appoints the superintendent, or general manager. This is not a political office, but a kind of technical superintendency. The officer is appointed for life or good behavior. He must be a scientific expert, acquainted with all systems of transportation at home and abroad. He is responsible only to the director, and is the only officer whom the director appoints.

This superintendent in turn appoints his immediate subordinates, such as foremen of the different divisions. And the foremen appoint the operatives. Appointments must, in all cases except the lowest, be made by way of promoting individuals who are already in the service. There is thus a regular gradation of responsibility. Every individual in the entire service is responsible to but one man, and that his immediate superior. Every individual is appointed for life or good behavior. Every individual, from the director down to the day-laborer, can be summarily dismissed from the service only by his immediate superior. But the only valid reasons for dismissal are incompetency and such insubordination as is injurious to the service. Every man dismissed has the right of public trial before a bench of judges composed, perhaps, of the mayor, the chairman of the city council, and the judge of the circuit court. This bench must summon witnesses, who must testify under oath, and the dismissed officer must be confronted by the superior who dismissed him. The bench of judges has power to affirm the removal or to reinstate the officer. Proceedings are to be public, and the press, public opinion, and the high standard of the judges, will see that justice is done.

Every appointee of the service should receive a pension after he reaches the age of sixty or sixty-five, according to the nature of his duties and the state of his health, as is done in fire departments. The fund for this pension should be contributed partly from a tax on the wages of employees, and partly from the income of the business. The prospect of this pension will be a noble incentive to integrity and efficiency.

Lastly, we have to-day the secret official ballot. This protects every employee in the freedom of his vote. He is not constrained to vote for the party in power in order to hold his place.

With a civil service like this there would not be the shadow of a charge of incompetency or corruption. Regulations even less complete render the fire service of American cities an enviable model. No one advocates a return to the days of private fire companies. With the public service conducted in like manner, all the advantages which I have sketched may be expected from public ownership of every public function. But without civil service reform it is better to go along as we are. The two must in truth come together. People will understand the need of the one as it comes with the other. And with public ownership of the monopolies, city government in America may be expected to take on generally a high plane of morals and efficiency. The best citizens would take greater interest than now. The poorest citizens would look upon themselves as sharers in the municipal prosperity. There would be no wealthy private corporations, dependent directly upon legislatures and councils, and compelled to resort to sinister influences. A new idea of what the city is for would become current, and with it a new kind of politics, a revived prosperity, and a happiness more widely diffused.

PROPORTIONAL
REPRESENTATION.

PROPORTIONAL REPRESENTATION.

THE legislature is the weak point in democratic government. The American people have succeeded fairly well in the organization of the executive, judicial, and administrative departments ; but their law-making bodies are a sickening failure. This applies to all grades of legislatures, — municipal, State, and federal. The name alderman is now a synonym for boodler and embezzler. To become a member of a legislature is understood in many States to be an invitation for bribes. The business interests of the country are reported to be in a gasp of agony as long as Congress is in session.

As might be expected, this distrust has shown itself in many and far-reaching constitutional changes. The powers of State and city legislatures have been clipped and trimmed and shorn until they offer no inducements to upright ambition. The powers of governors, mayors, administrative boards, and judges have been correspondingly increased. The growing popularity of the executive veto is one of the startling facts of the times. I know a city whose people turned out in mass-meeting to illuminate the heavens with bonfires in honor of a mayor's veto which had rescued them from outrages perpetrated by their own lawfully elected "city fathers."

The judiciary has gained materially at the expense of the legislatures, both in the express provisions of constitutions, and in the popular approval. Conscious of the feelings of the people, judges have steadily encroached upon the very fields of legislative discretion, and reluctantly, it may be, have more and more assumed the right to set aside legislative enactments. This has become boldly apparent in numerous recent decisions overthrowing such peculiarly political statutes as those which redistrict a state for the election of representatives. This interference of the judiciary, however justifiable the reasons, can only be fraught with danger to itself. It is thereby forced into the arena where are the heated questions of political expediency, at the expense of its integrity in the field where administration and justice alone are its sphere.

The statement is often made that representative government is a failure, especially in cities. But true representative government does not exist. We have a sham representation. It gives a show of fairness. But it is crude and essentially unfair. It does not represent the people. It represents the politicians. We are a law-abiding people. Yet our laws are made by a minority of the people, and by an irresponsible oligarchy more dangerous than that our fathers revolted against. The Congress which passed the McKinley bill did not represent the people. There was a Republican majority of three, but according to the popular vote there should have been a Democratic majority of seven. In the succeeding Congress there was supposed to be the most momentous upheaval in the history of American politics. The Democrats had a majority of 119 over all.

But had the people been represented this majority would have been only 39.   In the present Congress the Democrats have a majority of 79, whereas (taking the Presidential vote of 1892 as a basis) they should be in a minority of 29 ; the People's party should have 32 votes instead of 8, and the Republicans 152 instead of 129.   To call our Congress a representative body is the essence of sarcasm.   To mention two or three States, Indiana elects 13 Congressmen.   According to the popular vote they should stand 7 Democrats and 6 Republicans. According to the gerrymander they are 11 Democrats and only 2 Republicans.   In other words, every Hoosier Democrat whom you may meet has an influence on the legislation of his country equal to that of five and two-fifths Republicans.

In Iowa it goes the other way.   With 219,215 votes in 1892 the Republicans elected ten Congressmen, while the Democrats with 201,923 votes elected only one.   One Republican of that State is equal to nearly ten Democrats. In Maine 65,637 Republicans elect all the four

Congressmen, though the Democrats cast 55,778 votes. In Maryland and Texas the Democrats get them all; and in Kansas the Democrats have never had a representative since the birth of the State, though they cast from a third to two-fifths of the vote.

There is similar injustice in State and city legislatures. It is even more glaring than in the national legislature. In the latter there is a kind of counterpoise, since a gerrymander in a Democratic State is likely to be offset by another in a Republican State. But in a State legislature it goes all one way. Indiana in 1892, taking the presidential vote as a basis, should have elected to the lower house 48 Democrats, 46 Republicans, 4 Populists, and 2 Prohibitionists. She actually elected 63 Democrats and 37 Republicans. In the upper house the vote should have stood, Democrats 24, Republicans 23, Populists 2, Prohibitionists 1. Instead of this it was, Democrats 35, Republicans 15. Ohio elected 72 Republicans and 35 Democrats to the lower house. If the people had been truly represented, there would have been, 51 Republicans, 51 Democrats, 3 Prohibitionists, and 2 Populists.

I have mentioned the gerrymander. This animal is now attracting considerable attention. And he deserves it. Yet he is but a natural growth and a mere incident of the system of electing representatives in all parliamentary countries. This system requires a single representative, elected by a majority or a plurality vote, to stand for a limited territorial district. The district has no natural boundaries. It must, therefore, be artificially outlined by the legislature. The party in power does this in such a way that its own voters shall have small majorities in a large number of districts, and the opposite party large majorities in a small number of districts. The gerrymander is only an incident of the district system, and one of its minor faults at that. The system itself has become obsolete.

Public questions which in the thirteenth century, when our present system of representation originated, were only local and sectional, are now national questions. The early problem of representative government was, How to bring together into a single strong government widely separated localities, without destroying their local governments? It was the problem of federation. This problem has now been settled in all free nations.

Moreover, economic and social questions in those times were class questions. Mercantile law, import ánd export duties, were determined by representatives of the cities; the tenure of land by the military tenants; ecclesiastical law by the church assemblies. But to-day the organic nature of every great nation has made these into national questions of vital interest to every class and section. In the United States we have lately seen citizenship and the rights of property come under federal protection, and federal control has reached out for our two most influential business interests, — banking and railways. Federal interference will be much further extended when national trusts and syndicates become further consolidated.

In the earlier times there were several reasons why the district system fairly represented the electors and returned able representatives. There were no national political parties, since there were no national political questions. The earliest parties were divided on territorial lines. In England the Whigs were the city party, and the Tories the country party. Each representative therefore stood for a unanimous constituency. In both England and the colonies the legislature was the representative of the people united in opposition to a sovereign or his deputy. Political parties, as we understand them, are of recent origin. In the United States they are the growth of the last fifty years, and especially since the civil war have they made their marked advances. The peculiar feature of this development has been the supremacy of that new force in politics, the " machine." Party organization is an essential element of party government; but the extent, perfection, and detail of this organization in the United States is bewildering. It controls candidate and voters with an iron grip, and they glory in their subjection.

To-day the legislature, instead of being the

united representatives of those who protest against the government, is itself the government. Within its halls occur the conflicts for the control of the fortunes and destinies of the people. There is no outside enemy whose constant presence enforces harmony and mutual help. But two great parties, backed by their machines, stand face to face, and whichever masters the legislature, masters the people. The districts which elect representatives are no longer unanimous, but are usually quite equally divided between the two parties. Hence we have the disproportionate power of small aggressive factions with selfish interests holding the balance of power. Here is the long leverage of saloons, gamblers, and bribers.

The suffrage, too, has been widened. When a limited, local oligarchy selected a representative, it had all the freedom of choice which is exercised to-day in private business by the directors of a corporation in selecting managers, agents, and attorneys.

Again, legislation in the olden time was very meagre. The people were satisfied to live according to the customs of their ancestors. Government was simply a matter of administration; a representative system which could succeed then would fail now when legislation is the most intricate of arts, depending upon the profoundest of sciences, and dominating the most vital of human interests.

Lastly, the private corporation with its professional lobby was unknown fifty years ago. The lobby and the "machine" have grown up together like Siamese twins. The professional lobbyists are nearly always the managers of the political machine. They carry in their pockets the political fortunes of the legislators. The "third house" is the legislature. It is not surprising that a representative system which sufficed for an era of isolated, petty industries should wither and rot in a day of private corporations with public functions and fabulous resources.

Proportional representation is presented as a remedy, not only for the gerrymander, but also for the general collapse of legislatures. According to this reform, legislative districts electing single representatives, are to be abolished entirely. This is the primitive method unsuited to modern problems. Representatives are to be elected on a general ticket for the city, county, or State, as the case may be. Political parties or groups of voters equal to one per cent of the electorate may put in nomination a ticket or list of candidates containing as many names as they choose, up to the total number of representatives to be elected. The elector votes as at present with the Australian ballot. His votes count primarily for tickets, and not for individual candidates, but he may indicate his preferences for individuals on the ticket for which he votes. Should he scatter his votes among the candidates on different tickets, a vote for a candidate counts as a vote for the ticket on which the candidate figures, and any unexpressed votes are attributed to the ticket for which he votes as a whole. The returning officers determine first the number of votes given to each ticket; and the proportion which this vote bears to the total vote indicates the number of elected representatives

to which each ticket is entitled. The successful candidates are discovered by taking those
on each ticket who have the highest number of
preferences up to the total number of candidates
to which the respective tickets are entitled.

The principle involved, and at the same time
the very slight change from present methods,
can be shown by a table of votes for presidential electors. I have selected the State of
Indiana, and have taken the vote as given in
the fall of 1892, indicating the particular candidates by Roman numerals in the order in
which they stood on the respective tickets.

	DEM.	REP.	PEOPLE'S.	PROH.
I.	262,270*	255,615*	22,208	13,050
II.	260,661*	253,878*	21,861	12,830
III.	260,600*	253,836*	21,883	12,827
IV.	260,586*	253,815*	21,876	12,824
V.	260,580	253,799*	21,873	12,823
VI.	260,560	253,807*	21,873	12,821
VII.	260,588*	253,793	21,873	12,821
VIII.	260,547	253,808*	21,865	12,820
IX.	260,575	253,787	21,873	12,819
X.	260,600*	253,792	21,873	12,813
XI.	260,591*	253,777	21,871	12,820
XII.	260,590*	253,767	21,867	12,819
XIII.	260,581	253,767	21,867	12,815
XIV.	260,538	253,770	21,865	12,816
XV.	260,533	253,770	21,864	12,815
	3,910,390	3,808,791	328,392	192,533

Of course, under the existing system of majority (or rather plurality) rule, the 15 Democratic nominees are declared the successful candidates, seeing that individually each one receives more votes than any Republican candidate. But with proportional representation, *parties* rather than individuals must first receive their just deserts. Therefore the following calculation is made: —

Democratic	3,910,390
Republican	3,808,791
People's	328,392
Prohibition	192,533
TOTAL	8,240,106

$$8,240,106 \div 15 = 549,340.$$

Since there are 15 representatives to be elected, it would appear that every party should be entitled to one representative for every fifteenth part which it receives of the total vote cast for all parties. This quotient would be 549,340. But since the People's party cast only 61 % of this quotient, and the Prohibitionists only 33 %, they have not attained a fair electoral significance (say, 75 % of the quotient), and should be excluded altogether. The calculation would then proceed as follows : —

Democratic 3,910,390
Republican 3,808,791
                            ―――――――
                            7,719,181

7,718,181 ÷ 15 = 514,612 = electoral quotient.
3,910,390 ÷ 514,612 = 7 + remainder 308,106
3,808,791 ÷ 514,612 = 7 + remainder 206,507
         TOTAL,   14

The Democratic ticket, having the largest remainder, is entitled to the odd delegate, making a total representation of 8 Democrats and 7 Republicans.

It now remains to select the individual candidates on the several tickets. This is easily done by taking the 8 Democrats and 7 Republicans who show the highest number of individual votes. I have indicated these successful candidates by an asterisk. The fact that the 7 Republicans who are elected receive each a less number of votes than the 7 Democrats who are defeated may appear at first as a formal objection to the plan. But when we remember that it is *representation* of Republican and Democratic *voters* that we wish, and not primarily the success of candidates, the objection vanishes.

It will appear from the foregoing distribution of seats that the smaller the number of representatives to be elected, the more difficult it is to approach equality. Should the election have been held for the fifty members of the Indiana State Senate (the relative standing of parties remaining the same), the result would have been as follows, and the minority parties would not have been excluded : —

$$8,240,106 \div 50 = 164,805 = \text{electoral quotient.}$$

Democratic, $3,910,390 \div 164,805 = 23 +$ remainder $119,875$
Republican, $3,808,791 \div 164,805 = 23 +$ remainder $18,276$
People's, $328,392 \div 164,805 = 1 +$ remainder $163,587$
Prohibition, $192,533 \div 164,805 = 1 +$ remainder $27,728$

TOTAL,   48

There remain two senators to be assigned to the parties having the highest remainders. When this is done the Senate stands : —

Democrats	24
Republicans	23
Populists	2
Prohibitionists	1
TOTAL,	50

There are, indeed, various plans proposed for proportional representation besides the foregoing, but the differences are minor. They all agree in the abolition of districts, and the substitution of election at large. The arguments for the adoption of one will serve for all. In the first place, the gerrymander would become impossible. Mathematical justice between parties would be assured. But, more important than all, legislative bodies would be transformed from inefficient and corrupt bands of spoilsmen into capable, upright, and representative assemblies of law-makers. The power of the machine, the boss, and the lobby would be broken. Bribery would be rendered fruitless, and representative government would become what it has been only in name — free.

The secret of most of the evils under the modern highly organized political system is the factitious importance given to organized minorities and groups which hold the balance of power. This is the necessary result of a system which elects single public officers by a majority or plurality vote.

Now, plainly, as human nature happens to be constituted, very few men will "bolt" their party nominees, no matter how bad they may

be, when they know that the turn of a few
votes means the success of the opposite party.
Practically, there are never but two candidates
to choose between. A third party, except in
times of political earthquake, has no chance
whatever. Nothing to the American is so cul-
pable as " throwing his vote away." Consequently, the American way of bolting a ticket
is to stay at home ; and this only fortifies the
more the party machine.

Freedom from the rule of the machine means
first, power on the part of the voters to control the nominations of their party, and second,
power to defeat obnoxious candidates of their
own party without endangering the success of
the party.

Power to control nominations involves reform of the primaries and conventions. As it
is well known, these are in the hands of the
professionals, and here is the source of their
power. The main ground of machine rule in
primaries and conventions is the system of exclusive majority election. The chairman is
elected by a majority vote. He names com-

mittees, of course, only from the majority faction. Delegates, also, to conventions are elected only by the majority vote. This is wholly irrational. Why should a majority faction have all the delegates and the minority none? A simple device of proportional voting would remedy this serious evil. There would then be no "cut-and-dried" tickets. Anti-machine delegates and candidates could have some hope of nomination, and their supporters would have a motive for attending the primaries.

But suppose the elector finds that his party ticket has been put forward wholly in the interests of the party machine; that there is no candidate offered to him whom he deems worthy of election. Under the district system he must vote for the party nominee or else stay at home, or cast his vote in such a way as to benefit the opposite party. Proportional representation enables him to "bolt" the party ticket without bolting the party.

Of course, in order to do this, he must join with other protestants against the machine and nominate a new candidate and a new ticket. He can do this by petition, providing one per cent of the voters join him.

With all the tickets printed on the Australian ballot, the independent voter has now before him the ticket nominated by his party organization and another ticket of the same party nominated by petitioners outside the machine. Suppose he votes for the independent ticket. He does not endanger the success of his party as a whole, but only of one candidate out of the entire ticket; and he runs no risk of throwing his vote away, providing as many as a single quotient of the voters of the State cast their ballots with him. Under the district system his vote would be wasted unless the voters for the independent were a majority or a plurality of the voters in the district. In other words, the present system pens up a minority of independent voters in narrow districts under the whip of the party managers, but proportional representation tears down the fences, and enables them to combine throughout the State without risking the success of the opposing party.

The importance of a reform like this which would make the legislature independent and capable can hardly be exaggerated. We are living in a day of agitation for industrial and social reform, yet there is scarcely a reform proposed which does not sooner or later involve legislation. The legislature holds the purse, the life of the State. No wonder that in our country there is a marked tendency to deprive these bodies of even discretionary powers, and to bestow such powers on mayors, governors, judges, and administrative boards. Yet why should we expect anything better of our representatives when we make them the tools of local politicians, and when one-third to two-thirds of the members of city councils, State legislatures, and the national Congress are men serving their first term as law-makers?

It is not maintained that proportional representation alone would cure all our modern legislative ills. The late Professor de Laveleye, of Belgium, has well said that the remedies for partisan abuses in representative government are three: Proportional representation, secret ballot, and civil service reform. Indeed, these reforms are complementary and co-operative. The secret ballot has prepared the way for a simple application of proportional representation, giving the movement an advantage which it by no means possessed when it was ably advocated twenty-five years ago. Again, legislative reform of this kind is impossible in the presence of a spoils system. It would result in constant deadlocks. United States senators could no longer be elected by legislatures. But spoils are not the proper quest for law-makers.

With these three reforms co-operating there need be no fear of popular government. They are not make-shifts nor palliatives. They reach the sources of power. A reformed legislature would be the mightiest of engines for handling every other reform. It controls all other departments. It is nearest the people. With proportional representation it would include the best wisdom, integrity, and enterprise of the people. It would represent the opinions and wishes of the people in the same proportions in which they exist at large. It would be the people themselves in conference.   It would be a deliberative body in the truest sense, and not a side-show of puppets worked by the party machine and the lobby.   It would harmonize all social interests.   It would promote a spirit of compromise instead of partisan advantage. It would give power to the majority, a hearing to the minority, each in the persons of their ablest advocates.

HN 31 .C63 1967
Commons, John Rogers,
 1862-1945.
Social reform & the church